The Secret Life of Compost

A "How-to" & "Why" Guide to Composting —
Lawn, Garden, Feedlot or Farm

The Secret Life of Compost

A "How-to" & "Why" Guide to Composting —
Lawn, Garden, Feedlot or Farm

Malcolm Beck
with commentary by Charles Walters

Acres U.S.A.

The Secret Life of Compost

A "How-to" & "Why" Guide to Composting —
Lawn, Garden, Feedlot or Farm

Acres U.S.A.
P.O. Box 8800, Metairie, Louisiana 70011

Beck, Malcolm, 1936-
    The secret life of compost: a how-to & why guide to
composting-- lawn, garden, feedlot or farm / Malcolm Beck.
    p.cm.
    Includes index.
    ISBN 0-911311-53-X (hardcover)
    ISBN 0-911311-52-1 (trade paper)

    1. Compost   I. Title.

S661.B43 1997   631.8'75
                                             QBI96-40126

Library of Congress Catalog Card Number: 96-85733

Dedication

When I think back on all the work my family did to keep the farm and later the compost business going while I was off railroading, this book must be dedicated to my wife and five children.

My two oldest sons, Clayton and Malcolm John, hauled loads and loads of manure, waste hay and stable bedding from around the neighborhood, and they loaded it all by hand using ten-prong forks. They did get paid a small amount per load, but I think it was the excitement of getting to drive the trucks by themselves while most of their peers couldn't yet drive. The boys used old 3/4-ton pickup trucks with sideboards that could hold four cubic yards. On Saturdays they would make as many as 13 loads each.

When my two younger sons Robert and Russell were big enough to reach the pedals, we already had tractors with power steering and large dump trucks. The problem wasn't getting the boys to work, but keeping them out of the trucks and off the tractors so they could do their school homework.

Our youngest and only girl, Kay, followed her brothers in almost every respect and grew up pretty tough. However, she did mature into a beautiful young lady with an artistic touch, finally giving our business a little class.

And my dear wife, Delphine: to me she is wife, mate, best friend and business partner. To all the family — including daughters-in-law, son-in-law, nephew and all the other loyal employees — she plays the role of mother, grandmother, counselor, judge, jury, doctor, nurse and boss. And with all of that she still does her own housekeeping, cooking, and much of her gardening. Needless to say, without her there would never have been a Garden-Ville Organic Farm or Garden-Ville Compost Co.

My family is more than just help, they are also a source of inspiration. But the fires of inspiration were first started by J.I. Rodale and his publication Organic Gardening and Farming. Then it was Del Weniger, the great teacher and naturalist that was always there to answer or find answers to my many questions. Del was my mentor.

The fuel to continually keep the fires of inspiration burning has been supplied by Charles Walters, the many books he has authored and co-authored, his monthly publication, Acres U.S.A., and, finally, his agreeing to share a little of his vast knowledge and wisdom in this book.

Contents

Foreword

In the midst of what we call our "progress" an occasional person has the genius to combine solid ecological knowledge with technical skill and to apply the results with good common sense. We probably owe it to these persons that we are still here.

In the areas of soil building and maintenance and of the recycling of organic wastes, one of these leaders is Malcolm Beck, the author of this book. He has spent almost a lifetime in the study, experiment and practice which equip an inventive spirit to create new systems solving both old and new problems with our soils and our refuse.

Malcolm owned and ran Garden-Ville, a successful organic farm with its own marketing center, for decades. I enjoyed many delicious morsels from his fields. During all that time he conducted his own research on organic growing techniques, lectured widely on his discoveries in managing plants and soils, and published a book on insects in the organic garden. Gradually his interest focused on how to achieve and permanently maintain the finest soil quality. Soon that led him into much experimentation with composting. When he had applied much of the science and was well on the way to mastering the art of composting, we were all after him for his compost. He gave it to us until, in self defense, he had to start selling it.

Before long Malcolm had prepared a lot just for composting, and soon he was collecting the refuse from the stables, tree-trimmers and such, all around San Antonio in order to meet the demand for his compost. All the while he was studying about soils, experimenting with mixes, and designing bigger and better mixing machines. Nurserymen began to learn how great the soil mixes he was producing were, and soon he had a big business on his hands. I can remember when he had to begin importing bat guano from Mexico to meet the demand, as trucks which brought plants from California began to carry loads of his soil mixes all the way back to their growers out there.

Now his business in composting and selling soil mixes is so successful that it keeps a whole fleet of trucks on the roads and enriches countless flower pots, gardens, and whole fields. But Malcolm is not sitting back as a satisfied CEO. He is still studying, experimenting, and applying what he is learning. Beyond that, he has taken time to write down for all of us much of what he has learned about composting. So with this book any of us can do our own composting, grow better plants, or go into competition with him — because he's telling us his composting secrets!

— *Del Weniger*
Professor Emeritus of Biology
Our Lady of the Lake University

Overview

The beautiful planet on which we live is no more than a floating speck in the planetary system, one that is swung on a gravitational string in a 300-million-mile orbit around a nebular sun. It wobbles slightly on its axis so that on June 21 — in our northern hemisphere — summer arrives, plants grow and food is produced.

This little fleck of dust in the universe we romantically call Spaceship Earth is approximately 8,000 miles in diameter, 25,000 miles in circumference, and spins on its axis at over 1,000 miles an hour completing its rotation in 24 hours, giving each spot an equal amount of daylight and darkness.

Water covers 74% of this Earth. Only 20% is dry land. Out of this 20%, only 8% constitutes farm land, and only 3% is suitable for crop production.

Most of the passengers on Spaceship Earth are crowded into the seven breadbaskets of the world, half in Asia and the South Pacific, a fourth in Europe and Africa, and a sixth in North and South America.

In the United States this amounts to not even an acre per capita.

The great Greek philosopher Socrates called Planet Earth a gigantic organism, a concept Malcolm Beck expands upon in hauntingly beautiful epic style.

There is no pretentious prose in Beck's little opus: there is simply a humble recognition that a minuscule part does not command the organism, and that no one born of woman is smart enough to redesign nature. This harsh assessment comes terribly close to saying that modern agriculture is really not worth saving.

There is an oft-quoted poem the late William A. Albrecht liked to recite. Its sparkling lines explain the mindset of the modern agriculturalist and project the reason for being of a man like Malcolm.

This poem, author unknown, encapsulates what is really the message of this book. It tells with penetrating insight how men first fertilized the soil, and then . . .

At first men try with magic charm
To fertilize the earth,
To keep their flocks and herds from harm,
And bring new young to birth.

Then to capricious gods they turn
To save from fire or floods;
Their smoking sacrifices burn
On altars red with blood.

Next bold philosopher and sage
A settled plan decree,
and prove by thought or sacred page
What Nature ought to be.

But Nature smiles — A Sphinx-like smile—
Watching their little day
She waits in patience for a while
Their plans to dissolve away.

Then come those humbler men of heart
With no completed scheme,
Content to play a modest part,
To test, observe and dream.

Till out of chaos come in sight
Clear fragments of a whole —
Man, learning Nature's ways aright,
Obeying, can control.

The great design now glows afar;
But yet its changing scenes
Reveal not what the pieces are
Nor what the puzzle means.

And Nature smiles — still unconfessed
The secret thought she thinks —
Inscrutable she guards unguessed
The riddle of the Sphinx.

That man can lead only by obeying became the norm for Malcolm Beck when he started tiptoeing into the profession that acknowledges him as a leader. Living nature, not dead tomes, had the answer.

Malcolm Beck is a son of Texas, a pioneer possessed of great mental acuity and unillusioned self-sufficiency.

In cadenced lines worthy of J. Frank Dobie, fellow Texan Beck simply examines what everyone can see, leaving it to the reader to come to the appropriate conclusions.

As with other farmer-philosophers, he finds the origin of his calling in the laws of energy. Only readers intellectually uninspired can fail to see wasted energy as both an abomination and a lost birthright.

Here he becomes the lineal descendant of early environmentalists who made ecology a household word. In unrhymed yet poetic lines, Beck makes it clear that agriculture's waste of energy compounded many times its pollution and excesses.

Almost as if laying down planks on which tender-footed students could walk, Beck scans the horizons of science for clues that support the *finis* of his masterpiece, the compost pile, sweeter than Mother Earth herself.

His issues are not unlike those of the ancients — earth, air, fire and water. That the integrity of the earth's topsoil has been compromised is now copybook maxim.

John C. Cantillon, of Michigan State University at the time Malcolm Beck started his farming operation, clearly and succinctly stated the following proposition:

"The carbon, oxygen and nitrogen atoms that make up our bodies could have been of the bodies of soaring redwoods, stupid dinosaurs, graceful antelopes, and lowly sea slime. Reincarnation in this sense is a fact of life and death."

Agriculture today short-circuits some parts of the cycle. Nitrogen is being taken from the air by using electricity generated by fossil fuel in place of bacteria power. This modern breakthrough has enabled farmers to use nitrogen until pollution of the water supply has become a problem. Yet biologically correct agriculture requires something else.

"We have to loop the sewage system of the city to the farms," Cantillon said. And he might as well have added all the other products that become food for microbes in the fullness of time. "What is called pollution in the lakes and streams can be fertilizer on the farm. In a system where materials are continuously recycled, pollution does not exist."

Electricity generated by fossil fuels mean more than polluted streams and lakes.

Those who admit that fossil fuels cannot serve agriculture forever nowadays escape the horns of their argument by relying on atomic energy. Although the supply of atomic fuels is limited, this is not the real reason why our present state of stop-gap agriculture is bound to change. A premier issue in ecology makes the situation come clear.

Perhaps 300 million years ago, perhaps longer, this organism Earth was without oxygen. Anaerobic bacteria — that is, organisms lesser than the whole that live without air — started down the long path of manufacturing oxygen we use today. In time, green plants produced more oxygen by splitting the hydrogen atom of water from oxygen atoms. More and more organisms obeyed the divine injunction to increase and multiply. Then as now plants tied up carbon dioxide, using hydrogen atoms, and new compounds were built into plant tissues and oxygen was released to the air. Normally, when plants die, this operation reverses itself. Plants decay, and in the process oxygen is again tied up with carbon and carbon dioxide.

It is a generally accepted theory that millions of years ago, conditions existed wherein plants died and fell into shallow seas where there wasn't enough oxygen to support the bacteria life needed to rot them. Instead they were gradually buried by other sedimentation in the bowels of the earth until, under the agencies of heat and pressure, they became the coal and oil we now use. The important point to be considered is simply this. If all fossil fuel is dug up and burned, the earth returns to the primitive state of having no free oxygen. Ecological reasoning has it that since plants created all the free oxygen, it will take all the oxygen there is to burn that plant material.

The Earth organism that Socrates first described is a closed ecosystem. Only man's failure to find all the oil and coal can save him from self-destruction.

Ecologists and even editors know that most people take such pronouncements with a grain of salt. And yet the clouds of acrid smoke over the world's industrial centers are real.

America is sending up so much smoke and using so much oxygen that the United States already is borrowing oxygen from microscopic marine plants in the Pacific and the Gulf of Mexico — and even from over-populated and lower-fuel-consuming Asia.

These several considerations prompt us to ask what would happen if the Department of Agriculture's great expectations of exporting American farm technology to the so-called under-developed world became a reality. Ecologist Cantillon, mentioned earlier, put it this way: One, there might not be enough fossil fuels to support the mechanization an army of academic advisors now envision. The United States now imports sizeable amounts of fuels from under-mechanized countries — Latin America and the Arab nations. Southeast Asia, Africa and Southern Africa would have to do the same. Two, the resulting burning of these fuels would pollute the small envelope of air surrounding Planet Earth; and lower the amount of oxygen to dangerously low levels. Moreover, USDA's dream, if realized, would require the out-migration of some two billion people into already overcrowded cities.

Some of our exports — including varieties of rice — have a capacity for bringing instability to Asian agricultural economies. The paddy rice system is really an ecological marvel. To replace native varieties with the engineered plants our universities now supply would be a monument to the stupidity of man. Plants with higher potential for production seem also to carry in their genes a potential requirement for fertilizer needs, and rescue chemistry. The attempt to deal with bacterial, insect and fungal attack — and weed proliferation — soon visits mischief on workers who toil in the paddies and fish the canals. Pesticides not only annihilate a fair measure of the protein supply, they also destabilize human health. Our own experiences can be summoned to supply an answer to the question forming up everywhere.

Obviously the highly toxic organic phosphates poison the people, sometimes visiting instant death on the populace, sometimes damaging the proteins of the chromosomes, and in a broad-spectrum way infecting the gene pool.

Handing most of the world a bit more of our efficiency is something akin to handing it the plague. Rachel Carson was among the first to paint for us a picture that belonged in Dante's Inferno. Pests tend to develop immunity to pesticides, much as weeds suck in and give room and board to dangerous herbicide molecules. Plant diseases tend to evolve resistance mechanisms. When there are vast areas devoted to a single variety, there is precious little backup. During periods of outbreak this reduction of diversity bears consequences that run beyond instant comprehension.

When we examine modern agriculture in terms proposed by Malcolm Beck, our implied question is simply this: Is modern agriculture worth saving?

Well, strike the word "modern" as generally defined, and ask — "Is agriculture worth saving?"

Perhaps we should summon the testimony of Manfred Englemann, who was an ecologist in the Department of Natural Sciences, Michigan State University, when we first met up with his work.

We pour minerals, nitrogen, carbon, oxygen, hydrogen, phosphorus, potassium and sunlight into a funnel, he in effect said. The result comes out the bottom simply because most of the people live on 2% of the land. Farmers send this combination of minerals and energy to the city. In the city the food sponge full of minerals and energy ought to be wrung out so these values could be returned to the country.

Well, that isn't the way we do things.

In short, the agriculture we see in the American countryside is not very scientific. As it operates today, with monoculture corporation spreads and confinement chicken, pig and cattle operations, it is neither scientific nor economical. With pesticides, herbicides, low prices and a policy of attrition, it really isn't worth saving.

And yet there is a way for mankind to find and hold its place as part of Organism Earth.

The Earth is not made for man, the great Indian Chief Seattle said, *Man is made for the Earth*.

And the Earth's most precious tenants are those who till the earth in harmony with Nature. We now pass this inquiry into the hands of a doer of the word. — *Charles Walters*

Part I

The *Why* of Composting

Observe the Cycle of Life

Walk into the woods and meadows and visit with Nature. You will be in the presence of much life. Especially in the spring, you will find many types of plants, grass, trees, animals, and insects large and small. There will be life in abundance.

Now take a closer look. There is an equal amount of death, particularly in the winter. There will be dead grass and leaves, fallen limbs and trees, even dead animals and insects.

Every living thing will sooner or later die; no living creature, plant or animal, escapes death. In Nature, every dead thing is deposited in the very place it dies, and there it serves as a mulch protecting the soil until it finally decays and, in due time, is covered and replaced by still later deposits of expired life.

When a plant or animal dies, even though it may be consumed higher in the food chain, it will eventually be eaten by the decomposing microbes. They will decay or disassemble it and put it back into the soil. If they didn't, our planet would now be miles deep in dead things.

This life-death-decay cycle has built the thin layer of fertile soil that covers our land. It nourishes and grows our plants which are the bridge of life between the soil and man.

In the beginning, our planet was just a round mass of minerals moving in its planned orbit through space. At some point, the Almighty saw fit to breathe life onto earth, very meager and primitive life, but life with a crucial mission.

As these micro-forms of life lived and reproduced, they fed on and etched away at the rocky mineral earth surface, and as they died, their remains formed humus and mild acids to etch away still more minerals. This process went on and on until very small amounts of our first soil was formed.

Even though extremely small, the life, death, and decay of each preceding life form has been creating better conditions for future life forms. The decay process builds with added interest to the soil's bank account, and after countless centuries of creating conditions for higher and more complex forms of life, Man, the most complex of all life, was able to exist and be sustained.

Man . . . does he know? And can he trace his life support system far enough back to understand the life cycles? Man has accumulated much knowledge, but in areas of his healthy existence he seems to be slow to learn. Man sees death as a loss, or something to be sorrowful of, and he considers decay as something ugly. He doesn't understand why Nature always returns the dead back to the soil from where it came.

If man understood the laws of recycle and return, he would without delay put back into the farmlands all the animal manure and other organic waste he generates. He wouldn't be daily burying the thousands of tons of these life-generating materials in landfills that seal and lock them away from the natural soil-building processes for centuries to come.

In Nature, there is no waste. All is reused, and usually made into something of still greater value for the sustenance of life.

If man continues to break this law of return, he will not only stop the life-generating processes of the soil, he will actually cause the soil to degenerate. This process will sooner or later degrade all life . . . including man himself.

Why Recycle?

PLANET EARTH

Ours is the only planet known to support life. All life on Earth is maintained by a thin layer of soil covering a small portion of the earths surface. The quality of all life on this planet is determined by the quality of that thin layer of topsoil. If we allow the quality of that thin layer to degrade, all life on Earth, man included, will degrade to the same degree. The parent to all soil is mineral rock. The wind, rain, freezing and thawing break the rock into smaller sizes to start the soil-making process. Small rock particles do not become fertile soil until some life form has interacted with them.

The first life forms to attack the rock are microbes. They use elements from the air to grow and reproduce and slowly etch away at the rock surface. They exude, die and decompose, forming humus and mild acids on the rock, which dissolves mineral to further enrich the accumulating soil. This process goes on and on until higher plants and then animal life can be sustained. The death and decay of each life has a generating effect. Each time a living thing dies and decays on the soil, it creates a more fertile condition than was there before.

The energy to keep this cycle revved up comes from the sun. Plants alone have the ability to collect solar energy. Then, this energy passes through the food chain to all other life forms. Through the excrement and finally death of the many life forms, the sun's energy is passed to the soil to fuel the life systems in the soil and keep the cycle going so man, the highest form of life, can be sustained. Plants bridge the void between soil and man.

Walk onto the prairies or into the woods and look around, you will see much life, plant and animal, large and small. Then look down, you will see many expired life forms covering the soil. A mulch of dead things, twigs, leaves, grass, insects, manure, and even dead animals. Dig into this mulch and you will find it beginning to decay. The deeper you dig, the more advanced the decay until it fades into rich moist topsoil.

Nature has been building fertile topsoil by mulching and composting the surface of the earth since the beginning of time. With our modern way of living we consume, use, wear out and discard mountains of once-living materials. Most of this we waste by sealing it in landfills where it is locked away from its soil-building destiny for centuries to come. In the landfills, these natural resources are a waste. In the streams and lakes they are pollution. But on farmlands they become fertilizer. We must loop these natural resources back to food-producing soils so the life cycle can be maintained.

In the towns and cities, organic materials should be collected at feasible sites. Then through the art of composting these once-alive materials can be partly decayed to a condition that is sanitary and easy to transport to the countryside where Nature can reuse it.

Reports from governments of all countries, the United States included, show widespread humus depletion and topsoil erosion from the food-producing soils. The degraded soils can only grow degraded plants which forces the higher life forms to follow that same path. Only proper recycling of all organic materials coupled with good farming practices can stop and reverse this little noticed decline that creeps through all life.

FOOD PRODUCTION

Why doesn't man pay more attention to the natural chemistry, physics and biology of the world and see himself as part of that natural world, of its perfect design? Is it greed? Is it vanity? Or could it be that soil fertility has eroded to a level that no longer nourishes the body and the mind? Is man losing his ability to see and think logically ?

History books are full of stories about the decline and fall of many great nations. Soil decline was always the start of the fall. Poor soils result in failure of the economy and then the defense system. But if history were closely studied and the truth were known, you would find it was really decline of the mind that made the difference — and the mind begins to decline as soon as the soil begins to produce food that is empty of nutrients.

I know an animal nutritionist who taught at a small college. For an experiment he had his students divide a large group of pigeons equally into two separate large cages. One group was fed polished rice and water; the other group received brown, whole grain rice and water. Then he made the prediction that the pigeons on polished rice would get five degenerative diseases, stop reproducing and die prematurely.

He also predicted that the pigeons on the brown rice would remain healthy and live and reproduce normally.

His predictions came about exactly as he said, but the students learned something they weren't expecting. The first noticeable difference in the two groups was behavior. The pigeons on the polished rice became irritable and discontented and started to fight amongst themselves. The pigeons on the brown rice never became irritable or discontented.

This experiment inspired me to do a similar test. I used young chickens instead of pigeons and fed one group white bread and water. The other group received whole wheat bread and water. The results were the same as the test with the pigeons. The very first sign of malnutrition in the animals was irritability and discontent among those eating white bread and water. Those on the whole wheat bread always remained happy and contented. The first white bread-fed chicken died on the thirteenth day, and they were all dead by the seventeenth day. The chicks on whole wheat were kept on that diet until full-grown. They grew normally, never were sick or attacked by parasites. The hens started laying eggs, and we butchered the roosters.

Look at our society and the people all around the world. You can find many examples that show evidence of eating too much white rice and white bread. Or, could it be symptoms of soil decline!

SOIL MICROBES

Sir Albert Howard, the author of the book *The Soil and Health*, was an early scientist who recognized that the health of the soil determines the health of the plants, and the health of the animals that eat from them. Albert Howard is known as the father of compost. However, he learned from the Chinese.

They have been maintaining soil fertility for forty centuries. We have worn out farm after farm in two centuries.

When Howard first used compost around failing plants, he noticed almost miraculous recovery. The plants also became resistant to pests. He then fed animals from the composted, healthy plants and noticed they didn't contract diseases, even when allowed to mix with sick animals that had very contagious diseases. Health did indeed pass from one life to the next through the food chain. Perfectly healthy plants and animals have resistance to diseases.

Albert Howard believed his compost to be rich in nutrients but was disappointed when test returns showed it to be low in N, P and K (nitrogen, potassium and phosphorous). He had not used it thick enough to have good mulching effects, so he was eager to learn how a little compost could get such good results. After studying the roots of the plants with compost, he found the reasons. The beneficial root-colonizing microbes, especially the mycorrhizal fungi, were present in very high populations, and no harmful root pathogens were present. The roots of the nearby plants without compost were being attacked by pathogens and very few, if any, of the beneficial microbes were present.

I have a friend that grows cotton up in the high plains of Texas. He was slowly going broke, so he decided to look at other, and possibly better, ways than the conventional farming methods he was practicing. He cut his acreage from 2,500 to the 240 acres he owned. He then started using organic methods, among them biological sprays which included free-nitrogen-fixing microbes, which he applied along with feed-grade molasses for an energy source.

After a few years on the natural program, he discovered he could quit irrigating even though he was in a low-rainfall area. In drier years his production is below that of his irrigating neighbors, but his profit per acre is always greater since he has no irrigation or pesticide expenses. I have seen this man's cotton stand up showing no signs of stress while the neighbors cotton across a dirt road just 70 feet away under conventional farming methods was severely wilting, even though it had been irrigated twice that year. To find out how this was possible I had the soil and roots tested from both farms, and there was a striking difference. The roots from the organic farm had 24% mycorrhizal colonization with many spores and vesicles. The cotton roots from the conventional farm had only 2% colonization with some roots showing none. I discussed these two farms and the difference of soil microbes with Dr. Don Marks of Mycor Tech, Inc. and Dr. Jerry Parsons, our extension agent, and both agreed that overusing chemical fertilizers and pesticides on soils low in organic matter is detrimental to the beneficial soil life.

Mycorrhizal fungi form a symbiotic association with the roots of most plants. The fungi grow into or between the cells of the roots and use 10% of the carbohydrates the plant passes from the leaves to the roots. The fungi don't have chlorophyll in the presence of sunlight, so they can't manufacture carbohydrates. In return for the energy taken from the plant, the fungi grow out and search far and wide for nutrients and moisture and feed the plant so it can continue to manufacture more and more carbohydrate energy. The bigger and faster the plant grows, the farther and faster the fungi grow to feed the plant still better. A plant colonized with mycorrhizal fungi will have the equivalent of ten times more root. Another benefit of this association is that as long as the fungi are flourishing, they can prevent all root pathogens and damaging nematodes from attacking the root. Decaying organic materials on and in the soil keep both the plant and the fungi flourishing to help each other.

There are many beneficial forms of life in the soil. Scientists now tell us there is more tonnage of life and numbers of species in the soil than growing above. All of this life gets its energy from the sun. But only the green leaf plants have the ability to collect the sun's energy. All other life forms depend on the plant to pass energy to them. The plants above and soil life below depend on each other for their healthy existence and continued survival.

Another beneficial microbe that colonizes plant roots was introduced to me by Mr. Bill Kowalski of Natural Industries. He said he had a microbe that has been shown to knock out a half dozen root rots in the laboratory. At first I told him I was not interested unless it was known to stop cotton root rot, because the only deterrent to a booming apple industry in the hill country of Texas is cotton root rot. He replied it hadn't been tested on cotton root rot, but he would be glad to give me some if I wanted to try it.

Okra is related to cotton and back when we were farming we planted lots of okra. We had a spot on the farm where the plants suffered from cotton root rot. To test the new microbe, we planted two rows of okra across the root rot spot, then skipped two rows and planted two more rows of okra. The seed in these last two rows had been soaked in the product for a few minutes to ensure they would be inoculated with the microbe.

After the okra was in full production, Bill came over and we went out to inspect. Immediately we noticed the inoculated okra averaged a full twelve inches taller than the control rows. We walked down the control rows first and pulled up the smaller and weaker looking plants. We found the roots to be badly infected with some form of root rot and also full of root knot nematodes. Inspection of the inoculated row found not a single case of root rot or nematodes.

This was exciting. I immediately called Dr. Jerry Parsons. He came out and did his own inspection, and he too found lots of root rot and nematodes in the control rows but none in the inoculated rows. Then Dr. Parsons told us he had seen microbes such as these tested before and sometimes they worked perfectly, other times a little, and sometimes not at all.

I later contacted Dr. Don Crawford at the University of Idaho about this root rot-destroying microbe. Dr. Crawford originally discovered it. He tells me it is a saprophytic, rhizosphere-colonizing actinomycete, which means it is a microbe that lives on the roots and eats the skin sloughed off by a healthy, normal growing plant. As long as the plant is flourishing and the root is growing and lots of root skin is being shed to feed the actinomycete, it doesn't let a disease organism or root knot nematodes attack the plant roots.

The soil life and the plant life support each other. Dr. Parsons said the reasons these things don't always work is because the plants were probably growing so poorly they couldn't feed the beneficial root colonizer, allowing them to weaken; then the bad guys get a toehold. Hence the Laws of Nature: Destroy the weak and allow survival of the fittest. Without the colonizers feeding and protecting the plant, it falls victim to the natural laws. Weakened plants are attacked by all kinds of pests below and above ground. Nature wants the weak and sick plants to be destroyed. But man interferes. He uses his arsenal of pesticides to keep the unfit plants alive. Then he eats from the poisoned sick plants — and wonders why he gets sick.

The beneficial soil life can perform its job only if we do our part in following six important rules when growing plants.

RULES TO GROW BY:
1. Use the best adapted varieties for each environment.
2. Plant in preferred season.
3. Balance the mineral content of the soil.
4. Build and maintain the soil organic content — humus.
5. Do nothing to harm the beneficial soil life.
6. Consider troublesome insects and diseases as symptoms of one of the above rules having been violated.

Of the above rules, number 4 is the most important. It is the law of recycle and return. When practiced, it supports the other five rules and makes them less important. Because of rules 4 and 6 being ignored or not understood, the big use of pesticide became necessary. As a result, 1.9 billion pounds of pesticide are sold each year in this country.

We recognized and followed these rules on both of our farms. The first farm had a fruit orchard, an acre-and-half garden, and the rest was covered with pecan trees under which we grazed our milk cow and other farm animals. One day Dr. Sam Cotner, the vegetable specialist of Texas A&M, came for a visit. After looking around he said, "Beck, your farm is beautiful. Are you sure you are not using any modern farm chemicals?" I told him our little farm was more of a hobby than a necessity, as I made my living working on the railroad. As an experiment, we kept the farm all organic. He replied, "This is nice but it is not practical on large acreage. We have to feed the world."

The more I thought of Dr. Cotner's statement the more I realized a new challenge. We soon sold the little eleven-acre place and moved onto a much larger farm where we learned that the larger the area over which you have control, the easier organic farming becomes. You have more different environments to use, more room for rotation, and no close neighbors upsetting the natural balance with toxic sprays.

There are large farms all over the United States that have turned toward a more natural way of growing. And more are changing daily. Many are certified organic, following strict rules and using absolutely no harmful agricultural chemicals of any kind. The certified farms have a niche market and usually get better prices for their products.

In my travels around the country, and because of our business, I get a chance to visit with many farmers and ranchers that are changing or have changed to more natural, organic ways. When I ask what made them decide to change, the answer is always the same: "I was going broke following the modern, conventional ways."

Modern conventional farming is not all bad. It gives a lot of attention to NPK and other minerals needed to grow crops. But not enough importance is put on the soil life. Many agricultural pesticides and herbicides — and even some of the fertilizers — are harmful to soil life, especially when there isn't enough organic matter in the soil to supply the energy microbes and earthworms need.

Without this needed energy, the soil life can't properly process the applied minerals. The minerals may become imbalanced and toxic to the plants. The plants become weak. Then they can't feed the beneficial root colonizers. The colonizers can't furnish nutrients or protection to the roots. The plants get sicker. Nature wants to get rid of the sick plants and sends pests to attack and destroy them. Then the farmer is told to use toxic rescue chemistry. The environment, the farmer, and the consumer suffer. It is a vicious cycle. All become losers because of a lack of organic matter in the soil.

Organic materials from sewer plants, landfills, dumps, factories, feedlots and other sources become waste materials only after we have wasted them. In Nature nothing is wasted, she has no waste. When we recycle an organic product, it immediately becomes a natural resource. When organic resources are recycled back into the life stream, the whole environment comes out a winner. There are no losers. The soil life, plant life and animal life all gain tremendously. And all contribute to man's well-being so he wins the greatest.

Interlude

Creating Life & Death

Dante Alighieri, the Italian poet who gave the world *The Divine Comedy*, held a special place in Hell for the alchemists, who were the false scientists of his day. With crafty arrogance, and insulated from public scrutiny by hiding behind the complexities of their profession, they distorted not only Nature's God, but also God's handiwork as well. They were sentenced to perpetual torment, to wit:

The perpetual sentence handed off to Choco the Hog, a glutton, was mild compared to the fate of these falsifiers, the alchemists who falsified metals and became so adept at aping nature's secrets. They were punished by afflictions of every sense — darkness, stench, thirst, filth, loathsome diseases, and a screaming din. As in life they corrupted society by their falsification (in our time, bovine somatropin, carping ridicule of the compost art as unscientific, etc.), so in death these sinners are subjected to the sum of corruption, Dante's ever-present symbolism. The picture presented is one of what all society would be if falsifiers all succeeded.

Since falsification deceives the senses, even the body has no honesty. For by falsifying:

"You must know, unless my mortal multi-recollection stray,
How good and apt I was in falsifying nature's way."

The mindset of modern civilization no longer permits the entertainment of punishments such as those envisioned by the likes of Dante, but it allows crimes against Nature's God for which there seem to be no redemption.

And yet the mind of man towers above adversity.

That the Creator invented life is usually viewed as the crowning achievement of the Supreme Architect. But there is an even greater achievement, for God created death.

Everything that lives has to die, and everything that dies must be recycled, otherwise all the materials of Planet Earth would soon be used and tied up either in living things or those recently deceased.

The late Gene Poirot, the author of *Our Margin of Life*, put nature's requirements into these poetic lines.

> *Long before man could make a plow or a test tube,*
> *Nature was creating life, including man, and provid-*
> *ing an environment in which all life could live. She*
> *used the resources of air, water, sunshine and soil plant*
> *food minerals to make life. If She had created only life,*
> *these resources would soon have been tied up in living*
> *things, so She created death. This way resources could*
> *be recycled and used again and again. There is a basic*
> *law which says all life forms must give back at death*
> *what they took from the resources of the earth during*
> *their lifetime.*

Modern alchemists seek to cancel out divine injunctions by creating dangerous potions that resist the reason for being of the microbes. Thus the invention of plastics and pesticides, none of which makes fit food for microbes and therefore resists disintegration. Few will breakdown at all, and if sinister molecules become disassembled, they change the environment as breakdown products that are often more dangerous than the original.

But . . . dust thou art, and into dust thou shalt return. Andre Voisin, the great French scientist and farmer, called this oft-heard ejaculation a great scientific truth, one that ought to be emblazoned across the entrance of every academy of medicine in the world. It not only proclaims that dust of the soil — that is a mineral in trace form — is a necessary constituent of every cell, it also refines for us the idea that from life comes death, and from death comes life.

The mechanism that transforms death into new life is the compost system, and the agents of that transformation are the microorganisms. As with any organism, the micro-agents require a scientific diet for top-notch performance. They can perform — and do — on something less than the two-to-one carbon-nitrogen ratio, but they perform best when well fed.

The compost art that is described in the remaining chapters of this book relies on judgement, brains and maturity, and on taking an earth-bound situation by the nape of the neck and the seat of the pants, and shaking a result out of it.

So-called high-tech science is of little value in this endeavor, for high-tech applied to compost making is alchemy, a system that seems to argue with the sophists, "This is the case on which I base my facts."

The facts in our real world say that everything must be recycled in a time frame suitable to the head of the biotic pyramid, namely man. With the aid of billions of unpaid workers, we can take a hand in the process, assembling materials, preparing the meal for the microbial work crew, and allowing them to increase, multiply and die so that the soil and the environment can live.

In economics, a recycled raw material has to be treated as if it is newly arrived from nature, the source of all energy and matter. Thus the meltdown of scrap iron takes on the prime mover quality of iron ore from the Mesabi Range. It is new wealth, and not merely the transfer of value from one wallet to the next, as is the case with trade and gambling.

Much the same is true of all the materials that bow to the compost art. A slab of cement-like dung from a feedlot is merely a pollutant to water runoff, air quality, and a mountainous bill for the landfill or the man-made black mountains. Yet harvest of such materials and size reduction to enable microbial consumption turns such manures into brand-new value, much like the feed grains that grow out of the soil.

We can describe the work of the composter in detail, and timely acceptance of lessons taught can assure success in the compost craft.

Still, it seems, the compost art has an even greater task to perform, because it alone seems capable of teaching the world the true nature of accounting, bookkeeping, and value creation and transfer. Yes, all energy — kinetic to run the machines and metabolic to stoke the fires of the human dynamo — must come from the sun and its recovery instrument, the gigantic organism called Planet Earth.

A century or two ago, it was the common perception of mankind that it was impossible to damage, much less annihilate, the great energy-receiving instrument, Planet Earth. Early this century, Walter Lowdermilk of the U.S. Department of Agriculture totally destroyed that idea. He reported on the Middle East, desertification, the wasting away of resources, erosion, etc. He left an implied lesson behind. If puny man could so damage organism Earth, Earth the planet, and earth the farm, then those same puny hands harnessed to the task of restoration could salvage our soils equally well.

The Limits of Growth and *Beyond the Limits*, by Donella H. Meadows, *et al.*, both written in the last part of this century, iterate and reiterate the fundamental parts of the Lowdermilk findings.

These inventories of information suggest that the coming of age of the compost art is one of the most important developments of our times. They also suggest the mandatory nature of instructions in this book. At first glance it might seem that rescue of the garden plot with well-digested compost is one small step that is really too small when juxtaposed next to a problem of planetary proportions. Yet the composted garden calls into question the destructive technology unleashed because agronomists no longer remember that the anatomy of weed and insect control is seated in fertility management and not in dangerous alchemy from the devil's pantry. The windowbox lessons of yesteryear have now flowered into entire farms managed according to the simple compost instructions contained in this short manual.

Because of men and women like Malcolm Beck, grocery chains are now springing up, all dependent on the sort of management sanctified by compost made on the basis of uncommon good sense. The lessons that follow are so clear, they could easily make this book one of the most important to reach the shelves of eco-agriculture. — *Charles Walters*

Part II

The *How* of Composting

The Art of Composting

You can study science books until the biology, physics and chemistry of composting are well understood, but that doesn't make you a master. Composting is an art, and just like any other art, it can only be perfected by doing it and getting the feel of it. I knew nothing about the sciences that explain what happens in compost, but I learned to make compost by watching things decay in Nature. Then gradually, over time, I began to understand the processes involved.

When I was a curious child between the ages of two and five, we lived at a place that had a barn with a solid wooden fence running parallel to the east wall. Between the wall and the fence was an area four feet wide. In that little lane were some big hackberry trees. The leaves blown by the wind collected between the barn and that fence up to fourteen inches deep. That was one of my favorite places to play. It always smelled so good! I hoped the leaves would eventually build up so high that I could see over the fence, but I noticed every year before the leaves would start falling again, the pile would be way down and the new falling leaves would only bring the pile up to the original height. I would always dig into this leaf pile and find all kinds of neat bugs and worms to play with. It was always nice and moist, even if it had not rained in a long time. I also noticed how the leaves gradually changed into soil and tree roots were always growing up out of the ground into the decaying leaves. Childhood reasoning told me the roots were eating and drinking from those decaying leaves. By the young age of five, Nature had taught me the secret of her life cycles.

Once I got a little bigger, handling manure and other farm waste was always a part of my life. It was a necessary farm chore, and I didn't mind it any more than any other chore. I could easily see the rewards of hauling the waste back to the fields. The crops were always bigger in the area where it was applied, more earthworms were there, and the soil was softer and easier to plow.

Many books on composting make it so complicated that you need advanced degrees in science to understand them. Most people who successfully make compost, however, learned by observing Nature. It is much easier to understand the science after you have mastered the art of composting than the other way around. Studying the science first seems to dampen the desire to experiment. You try to make something work that doesn't, because you are unaware of some factor that wasn't covered in the books. Then you become frustrated. Much of the material written on composting is by people that studied the book sciences, but I am not sure they conferred with Nature as to when, where and how it should be done.

ECONOMICS AND NATURE

If you study Nature, you soon learn she is very thrifty. She doesn't make an unnecessary move or process. Nature never wastes energy while she recycles expired life. "The Law of Least Effort" was written by her. We need to study all her laws and learn from her. In Nature, every dead thing is deposited in the very place it dies and there it serves as a mulch protecting the soil until it finally decays and, in due time, is covered and replaced by still more dead things. As these dead things are disassembled by the microbes, the proteins are changed into ammonia gas. Some of the gases are used by the microbes, some are turned into nitrates, a small amount is used by growing plants, and any ammonia not used is absorbed into clay and humus in the soil and held for future plant use. Little if any escapes to the air.

Carbon dioxide is also released as the microbes break down organic matter. Carbon dioxide release is most abundant in warm weather when plant growth is greatest. The carbon dioxide drifts up from the soil surface and is captured by the leaf surface of the many plants growing above. Again, little escapes to the air and what does goes over to feed plants that are growing in areas that don't have decay processes going on under them. The plants take the carbon out of the CO_2, use it for food and release the oxygen.

Some scientists are saying an excess amount of carbon dioxide (CO_2) in the atmosphere is causing global warming. But science has also proven an abundance of CO_2 in the air allows plants to more efficiently use water and grow better. I believe global warming is being caused by humans uncovering and creating too much bare soil through some of our agricultural practices, herbicides and paving over. My own testing has shown bare soil in full sun to be 35 degrees warmer than nearby soil under mulch or plant cover.

Mulch also protects the soil from heavy rain drops that settle soil particles together to form an impervious crust. The broken-up water droplets filter through the decaying mulch and collect the nutrients released by the microbes and slowly carry them to the roots of plants, or back into the life cycle.

The layer of mulch also keeps the moisture from moving up and evaporating into the air. As water moves upward in the soil, it carries dissolved minerals with it. When the water evaporates, it leaves the minerals concentrated at the soil surface as salts which form a crust through which seeds can't sprout and plants can't grow. With the evaporation stopped by mulching, the moisture and minerals stay dispersed in the soil for root collection.

UN-ECONOMICS OF MAN

Nature does not agree with some of our wasteful composting ways. We allow moisture, ammonia and carbon dioxide to dissipate into the air. And we waste energy while doing it. Nature decomposes dead things and manure right where they fall. The organic material decays and nourishes new life in that area. If small amounts of nutrients happen to escape that area, it is because the rains carried some off to feed the life in the streams, lakes and the oceans.

Many times, because people take the Not In My Backyard (NIMBY) approach to composting, raw materials have to be hauled great distances to a remote location before composting is allowed. Nature isn't given any consideration. The pollution from noise, from tire, gear, and brake wear, and from engine and crankcase exhaust nullifies much of the good done by composting.

I have visited many compost operations and found some very inefficient. They use up more energy to make compost than it contains when it is finished. My dry weight compost contains about 5% mineral and 95% energy, you can burn it and measure the Btu's just like gas, oil or coal, since they too were plant life in past times. You gain nothing and Nature loses if you burn up as much or more energy than the compost contains when you get through making it. This energy is the most valuable part of the compost, the soil's greatest need. The rest of the soil's needs can, temporarily, be bought in bags. With continued use of compost the need for bagged fertilizers will go down until eventually little, if any, is needed.

A good example of how inefficient some composters are: Once in the past a compost company moved near San Antonio and set up operation at a big feedlot. Then they discovered I was in the composting business. They were fine ethical people, so they came to me and asked if we could get along. They assured me that they would not cut my prices. We quickly became friends and visited each other's locations and exchanged ideas and experiences. On visiting their operation I saw they were composting in an insulated house. The operator bragged it took them only seven days to make compost. It took me six to seven months. This was hard for me to accept, but it so happened that my visit was on the seventh day. He opened the doors and sure enough he had a fine looking compost.

My immediate thoughts were that I need to check into this. Then another thought struck. That house only held seventy yards. He was limited to making ten yards per day. He also told me their construction time from start to finish on the building was almost six months. And before they could load the house, the material had to be ground to proper size; the carbon-nitrogen ratio had to be perfect and the moisture just right. Once the doors were closed, a switch was turned on and the computer-operated blowers took over to keep temperature, oxygen and whatever just right by blowing air up through the floor. This was all great, but all that energy and high technology just to let something rot? If I dumped two hundred cubic yards on the ground the day he started construction and turned it four times, like I normally do, we would both have our first compost to sell on the same day. If I continued to make 200 yards each day, six days a week, I would have 200 yards (minus the shrinkage per day) to sell, and he would still only have his 10 yards per day.

I was honest and told him his operation wouldn't fly. It didn't. Three separate operators tried before it was finally shut down for good. Now the building is being used to store hay. A very expensive barn. They never seemed to figure it out. All that expense and energy spent just to make 10 cubic yards per day.

The micro- and macro-life forms do the never-ending work of the decaying/composting for us. And like any other living entity, they need water to drink, air (oxygen) to breath, carbon (carbohydrates) for energy and protein (nitrogen) to build their bodies. They also need minerals, but the carbon and nitrogen materials being composted contain these minerals since they too were alive at one time. The moisture, air, carbon and nitrogen need to be blended and mixed in a way to create the perfect hotel/factory/cafeteria to keep the decomposers comfortable and happy so they can work, eat and multiply. The compost pile itself is their hotel. They don't need an additional high-tech, expensive building that man has designed for them to work in. They will work in these high-tech contraptions and work well, but if we don't watch it we may end up with a bunch of spoiled microbes that will become lazy and soon demand welfare.

Home Garden Recycling

Home gardeners have many more options than the commercial composter or the farmer. Unlike the big guys, the gardener does not have to think in terms of economics of energy spent. The home gardener is not paying wages, burning diesel fuel or wearing out expensive equipment. All the work put into composting can be chalked up as much-needed exercise and mental relaxation. The gardener just needs to pay attention to Nature, recycle and make sure he or she doesn't waste soil nutrients and cause pollution.

Most importantly, don't get bogged down following fancy and complicated recipes and formulas unless you enjoy being scientific. Keep it fun. You can only be a help to Nature when you do something you enjoy.

The three most important things the home gardener needs when learning to make compost are:

1. A willingness to experiment with blending carbon and nitrogen materials.

2. Learning the correct moisture content and air space.

3. The patience to let the microbes do their disassembling job.

No matter what you do or mistakes you make, sooner or later it will all decay anyway.

CARBON (C) MATERIALS

Sometimes called brown or bulking materials, they are: sawdust, wood chips, bark, straw, dried leaves, dry grass, corn cobs, shucks, dry corn stocks, seed hulls, cardboard, paper, dry cane and grass hay. Legume hay is pretty high in nitrogen and could be used either way. All organic, compostable materials contain carbon and some nitrogen but some contain more nitrogen than others.

NITROGEN (N) MATERIALS

Also called green materials, nitrogen sources consist of: all manures fresh or dried, all green plant life such as grass, leaves and weeds, all seed meal such as cotton seed, guar seed and soybean seed. All animal products such as blood meal, meat and bone meal, leather meal, hoof and horn meal, meat scraps and feathers. Kitchen and food waste would also be nitrogen materials.

If not sure whether the materials you have are high in carbon or in nitrogen, there is an easy test. Just put the material in a pile, and if it is dry, wet it. If nothing seems to happen, it is carbon. If it quickly starts to stink and draw flies, it is definitely high in nitrogen.

In the many talks I give on composting, I always suggest using at least a small amount of manure to give compost the best quality. The question that is always asked is, "What is the best type of manure?" After years of using almost every manure found in Texas, I have concluded that the best is the type that is nearest, most abundant and easiest to get. And that includes dog and cat manure. At one time I had a neighbor that raised hunting hounds. Periodically he would clean out his dog pens and would bring me a pickup load of dog manure. I composted it along with my other materials. Because of the bones the dogs ate I felt their manure added extra phosphorus, it must have. That was on the first farm at which there was a phosphorus deficiency. The crops where that compost was used did great.

However, many books and experts say don't compost dog and cat manure because it may carry diseases and parasites that can be contagious to man. Most people I know have a dog or cat or both and they all poop. I personally don't know of a single case of infection but it probably has happened. You can even get diseases and/or parasites from shaking hands with someone, but, we still do it. The books and experts also tell you not to compost diseased plants, but rather put them in the garbage along with the dog and cat manure.

A good, well-made compost pile is the best place to pasteurize these nitrogen-rich materials. It recycles them and turns them into something valuable. Letting the garbage truck haul them away only moves them from one place to another, which wastes transportation and the materials — and they will not be pasteurized.

All manures are a good nitrogen source, but considered not clean and should be handled as such. However, composting them with carbon materials is nature's way of cleaning them up and making a perfect plant food of them.

MINERALS

All life forms need minerals, including the microbes that help your compost decompose, but you need not worry about them. They will find the minerals they need in the material being composted, because it too was alive at one time.

If soil test or plant symptoms indicate a mineral deficiency, especially in alkaline soils, it is always best to add the mineral needed to the compost while composting. The microbes will digest the mineral and add it to their bodies which chelates it or keeps it from locking up in alkaline environments. The minerals from the microbe exudate always remain available for plant uptake.

PARTICLE SIZE

The smaller you can chop up the composting material — using a lawn mower, small grinder or machete — the better. The smaller the particle, the more surface area for the microbes to work on. Also, a small particle size holds moisture better in the small, home compost pile.

LOCATION

Where should the home gardener compost? Anywhere he or she wants to! The material will rot in the sun, shade or in the living room, but it is best to keep it out of sight of a nosy neighbor. You may have one of the few who can smell with their eyes. If you can help it, don't put your pile where water can run off a roof onto it or in a ditch where it will wash away. You may compost on a slab and then catch the leachates (compost tea), or put it on the soil so earthworms can work their way up into it, which is good. If a tree is nearby, its roots will also find the pile and grow into it. To stop the roots before they get too big, just move the pile over to a bare spot each time the pile could use a turning.

CONTAINER

Should the gardener use an enclosed container or open pile? Again, suit yourself; it will rot either way. Many gardeners just use an open pile; some enclose three sides with pallets, bales of hay, bricks, etc. Small-mesh wire cages are probably the most popular. If you are a gadget person, there are all types of fancy containers on the market. They all work, but their miniature in-vessel methods might take some experimenting in the beginning.

EARTHWORMS

If you don't have enough carbon materials to compost or just don't want to compost but still want to save your kitchen scraps, let the earthworms eat it. They love kitchen scraps. Each earthworm can eat half its weight in scraps each day, turning it into the finest, richest, most perfect soil known to man. Just bury your kitchen scraps for them a little at a time each day in the flower beds, garden or around shrubs. Don't bury the scraps deep, but make sure they have ample soil cover to keep flies from breeding or pets from scratching them out. If it is bad weather or you don't have time on certain days to do this worm feeding, refrigerate the scraps until you do.

You can even compost in a worm box just outside your door. In northern climates where it really gets cold and the soil freezes, put the worm box in your garage or basement. Make a box 1 ft. deep, 2 to 3 ft. wide, 3 to 4 ft. long, and put a good wooden lid on it to keep rodents, pets and flies out. If placed inside, put a waterproof bottom in it and a couple inches of garden soil. If outside, no bottom is needed, but bury the sides 2 to 3 inches in the soil. It is always best to chop or grind kitchen scraps into small pieces before feeding them to the worms. Not all worms are suited to eat scraps. You may need to get a start from another worm composter or find some advertised in garden magazines. I have always played with worms and watched other people worm compost, but I am definitely no authority on so-called *vermi*composting. There are books on worm composting that go into greater detail.

Earthworms are very important for a healthy soil. Charles Darwin studied earthworms for 50 years and finally concluded, "Without earthworms, the vegetation in many parts of the world would degenerate to the vanishing point."

Earthworms are an indicator of healthy soil. In my younger days I loved to play in freshly plowed ground. The fresh-turned soil smelled so good, and the feel of moist, soft soil to my bare feet was so invigorating. Many times I would follow right behind the mules or tractor so I could watch the limitless number of turned-up worms wiggle back into the soil.

In those years, other than for fish bait, I didn't understand the worms' real value. I am glad these memories are so vivid, because now it is rare to follow behind a plow and find either earthworms or even the good soil smell.

Earthworms tunnel as deep as six feet, bringing up minerals from that depth. In comparing worm castings with the surrounding soil, they are found to be five times richer in nitrogen, twice as rich in calcium, twice as rich in magnesium, seven times as rich in phosphorus, and eleven times as rich in potassium. Along with these five minerals, the trace elements needed for plant growth are also present in the castings, and all of the minerals are readily available for plant use.

Earthworm tunnels allow rain water to quickly penetrate the soil. The tunnels aerate the soil, allowing oxygen to easily penetrate, and soil gases — carbon dioxide and methane — to escape. When earthworms are present, beneficial soil microorganisms are increased seven times or more, while harmful microbes and nematodes are destroyed as they pass through the worms' digestive systems.

Earthworms will not and cannot live in a soil void of organic matter. Do your part and build up the soil's organic content and the earthworms will build the fertility to perfection.

If you don't the have desire or time to compost or feed worms, your kitchen scraps would make a nice gift to a friend or close neighbor who is an avid composter. It is a sin against Nature to waste clean kitchen scraps down the drain — at least until all communities are composting the sludge from their sewer systems.

The Chemical vs. Natural
Farming Debate

Most all farm produce — meat, fiber, vegetables and grain — is sent into cities where it is processed and consumed and eventually ends up in some form of garbage or sludge. A small amount may be composted and used in gardens or the landscape in urban areas. Little, if any, makes it back to the farm from whence it came, where it is most needed, and where it belongs. Somehow, with the invention of modern farm chemicals, our human logic (or was it greed?) told us it was no longer worth the effort to recycle the organic materials back to the land. It would be OK, and even more modern and sanitary, to waste it in landfills. Most industry and agricultural universities jumped on this chemical bandwagon. But there were a few people who understood natural soil fertility and warned of the dangers of wasting and not recycling. Instead of consulting Nature to see what she recommended, we used human brilliance and the organic-versus-chemical feud started.

The chemical industry, with its mountains of grant money, is able to yell the loudest. While we argue, Nature is being neglected and abused, but we can ignore and abuse her only so long. Sooner or later, for our own sake, she rebels and starts showing us the problems. When we don't heed her warnings, our environment continues to degrade. Few people realize that it is also the quality of the soil that determines the quality of the water we drink and the air we breathe.

The guilty are on both sides. Neither the chemical nor the organic supporters are willing to ask Nature's approval of the other method. The chemical side abuses the soil with more and more out-of-balance soluble minerals that lack the carbon energy to fuel the microbes necessary to make good plant food. Without the humus to provide energy, the pure chemicals cause imbalance in the plants. The result is weakened plants that invite pests. Then rescue chemistry, mostly toxic, is used to try to solve the problem. Without organic energy in the soil, the decomposing microbes can't degrade the toxins or even tolerate them, and they too are weakened and die. The end result is that the soil becomes poisoned and dead.

Some organic proponents would like to see all agricultural chemicals abandoned regardless of their potential benefits. Most people, organic enthusiasts included, consider compost low in nitrogen. But low nitrogen is all Nature needs. Besides, Nature puts microbes in compost that are free-nitrogen fixers. They don't need legumes to support them; they use energy from the compost to take nitrogen directly from the air. The atmosphere enveloping Planet Earth contains 78% nitrogen; it's there for our use. Why buy nitrogen? In the laboratory, these nitrogen-fixing microbes captured the equivalent of 1,000 lbs. of nitrogen per acre in a ten-week period when they were fed carbohydrates for energy on a weekly basis. (Louis M. Thompson, *Soil and Soil Science*, 1952).

Ten to forty tons of compost per acre are often recommended to meet crop nitrogen needs. Nature doesn't ask for these high volumes, because with time she will take the correct nitrogen needs from the air above, if we only supply the energy. In most cases transportation alone would make hauling large volumes of compost to farm acres prohibitive. Farm soils still in fair condition can benefit from a combination of compost and good-quality agricultural chemicals. By adding a relatively small amount of compost (1-2 tons per acre) when fertilizing, the farmer will see increased production. The results seen from this method would quickly get mainstream agriculture to accept and eventually demand more compost.

Even at two tons (4-5 cubic yards) per acre, some farmers would be financially burdened to transport, spread and pay for compost. Everyone benefits when our food-producing soils are improved. There have been and still are many tax-supported programs to help farmers. Some have been questionable. An incentive for the farmer to increase the organic content of the soil would be the most sensible approach. The farmer could grow cover crops instead of cash crops, or he could spread compost if he wanted to keep the fields in production while he built the organic content. Another incentive that would be good for the farmer and benefit everyone is to pay for quality rather than quantity of production. The farmer who is well-compensated for high-quality produce will be more able to maintain soil quality. Compost is the shortest route to quality.

If compost is so needed on farm acres, why, you may ask, am I selling and promoting compost in the cities? Because that is where the masses and consumers live. When they see the excellent results of using compost in the landscape and on the vegetable garden and taste the quality of compost-grown produce, they will be convinced. When they realize that compost reduces the need for irrigation and pesticides, the city folks will better understand agriculture. It is their vote that will encourage lawmakers to enact laws for a sound ecology. Voters will help pass and support laws for better education about Nature, how she works, and the value and importance of healthy, living soils. Until the consumer understands and demands fertile soils and healthy foods, it will be hard to break the farmer away from relying on and overusing chemicals. This is especially true because most agricultural publications are dominated by chemical journalism and advertisement. Our agricultural universities go along with the chemical philosophy. They downplay manures and compost for fear of jeopardizing the grant money provided by chemical companies. At the moment, no compost company, public or private, could survive relying on an agricultural market alone.

Building Soil on the Farm

Think simple, economical and natural.

Study the forest floor. Nature doesn't compost materials in a pile before she uses them. You need not either unless you want to get rid of noxious weed seeds, pathogens or reduce the volume and weight so it can be hauled a greater distance. Composting for a short time with few turnings will accomplish this. It is best to let as much of the composting activity as possible be completed in the soil.

Orchards, vineyards, and other perennials are crops that benefit from composting materials before they are put around the plants. Even in those areas, you don't need the finished quality you would sell in the city.

If you need to hold manure for several months for some reason, pile it up in a way and in locations where it can't soak up a lot of water. Some of the best vegetables I ever grew were with cow manure mixed with a little cane hay that was stored in a big pile. The manure was from the stockyards. It had been accumulating for more than a year. They were adding a couple yards daily, pushing the pile up high with a crawler tractor. It did still smell like cow manure. However, cow manure is not an offensive odor unless it is from feedlots. Range-fed animal manure does not smell bad.

Manure from feedlots is a lot higher in protein, which makes it higher in nitrogen. The high protein causes it to smell worse. You may want to compost it to get rid of the odor, but don't waste a lot of time and energy to get rid of something the soil life doesn't mind having.

Concentrate on getting all manure, spoiled feed, hay, feathers, cobs, hulls, gin waste, ashes, and other organic materials back to the land the most economical and easiest way possible. Spread it thin and disk-in shallow. It is important to mix moist manure into the soil quickly, because as it loses moisture to the air, it is also losing ammonia nitrogen at the same time. You want the ammonia absorbed onto the clay and humus of the soil where it is stored for future microbe and plant use.

It is best to apply manure and other organic waste on the stubble as soon as the crops are harvested. Don't drive in the fields when they are wet because that will cause soil compaction. Annual light applications of one to five tons per acre is much better than one heavy application.

Heavy applications can upset the biology and chemistry of the soil for the next crop, unless it is a cover crop that will be turned back for soil building. Heavy applications could possibly cause ground water and surface water pollution if heavy rains came before the soil life had a chance to digest the manure and other organic material.

When using feedlot, dairy, turkey and chicken manure, get a periodic soil test to make sure you are not overloading your soil with a salt, arsenic, potassium or phosphate. Some of these minerals are really pushed through animals kept in confinement. Manure from range-fed animals is rarely a problem.

If you are a weekend hobby farmer, it isn't so important how and when you handle organic materials as long as you handle them properly and don't pollute. But if you farm for a living, it is most important that you think about economics and don't waste time, work, fuel or nutrients when getting organic materials back to the land. The best advice I can give is to always observe Nature. She can teach you things that the books, the Ph.D.'s and I don't know.

COVER CROPPING

When compost isn't available, the soil can still be improved organically. I had to do this on my second farm. When I purchased it in 1968, the soil was so poor that in a good year, Johnsongrass would only get knee high. The previous owner had planted oats, and when they finally headed out, they were all of ankle tall. We put in a garden; the plants came up and stopped. The soil was yellowish red in color and real sticky. During rains, most of the water ran off, and the soil would soon be dry. In some areas we set up an irrigation system and sprinkled slowly, trying to get moisture deeper into the soil. When we finally went out to move the pipe and sprinklers, we bogged down to our knees. We had to go barefooted. You couldn't wear rubber boots, the suction would hold them in the ground.

We had the privilege of a visit from Robert Rodale of *Organic Gardening* magazine shortly after we moved to that farm. After showing Bob around, I asked him what would be the best way to bring soil fertility up short of hauling in a lot of compost. (I had neither the compost or the money to buy it to cover all the farm.) Bob thought for a moment then said,

"The land is level, you don't have bad erosion. The soil is clay, so it is probably holding nutrients, but the alkalinity has them locked up. What you need is to get life into the soil with organic matter."

With money short, I decided against planting cover crops for a while. I just let the weeds grow, and as soon as they got up in full bloom I would mow them off with a cycle bar. I did that for two years. Then I decided to try Sudangrass. I spread the seed with a cyclone and ran over it with a light disk. There was so much organic matter from the mowed weeds that it didn't do much of a job covering; however, I did get a fair stand. Now I had Sudan and weeds to mow down. I mowed twice. It was now fall so I decided to try a winter legume. I didn't know much about legumes. When the seed company asked what type I wanted, I said, "Give me the biggest."

I went home with scarified hubam clover seed and an inoculant to put on it. Again I used the light disk harrow to shake the seed through the now-heavy layer of mulch that wasn't rotting for lack of nitrogen and soil life. Luckily soon after planting, a rainy spell set in and up came every seed. It was the ideal environment for clover — calcium-rich soil, heavy mulch and little competition from other plants because of low nitrogen. That hubam clover didn't quit growing until it was over eight feet tall. People came from miles around to see it. Among the sightseers was a botany professor from a local university. He took pictures, then told me that was the last good clover crop I could make on that spot but he couldn't tell me why, other than that is what the old timers had told him.

We made good money from selling clover seed. Because it was a crop that the deer wouldn't eat up, I had to try clover again. And just like the professor said, I didn't make another good clover crop. But I did find out why. The clover did such a good job of breaking up the hard soil, putting in nitrogen, releasing minerals, and building fertility that it was a good environment for seeds of every type that had been waiting in the soil for years for just this condition to sprout and grow. There was too much competition for the clover.

By now we were making quite a bit of compost, enough for the upper five acres of our truck garden area. But compost sales were picking up, so little went to the farm. We continued to use cover crops. We tried alfalfa but learned in a hurry it was bad news because of cotton root rot. Instead, we used annual-type winter legumes mixed with rye. Lana vetch and elbon rye was our favorite combination. The rye, being a grass with a massive root that also destroyed root knot nematodes, fed shallow and used nitrogen from the soil. The vetch had a deeper root, pulling up moisture and nutrients from deep while getting its nitrogen from the air. This made the combination an excellent cover crop — they were compatible. As the rye used up the nitrogen in the soil, it forced the nitrogen-fixing microbes in the root nodules of the vetch to take most of its nitrogen from the air. In the end, you would get more poundage of nitrogen and tonnage of green matter per acre than if you had the rye or vetch alone.

Animal breeding problems and soil tests told us we were short on phosphorus. Otherwise, our soil fertility had improved dramatically and looked good. After proper colloidal rock phosphate applications, we found the vegetable production was almost the same in the cover-cropped area as in the composted area. We used no other fertilizer.

Comparing the composted area to the cover crop area, we learned that both methods will get you where you want to be.

If you are impatient, compost gets fertility up the quickest, but it will usually cost more. Cover cropping takes much longer. Compost brings in minerals. Cover crops can only make available the existing soil minerals.

Good fertility management would make use of both compost and cover crops and keep the soil healthy and productive forever. Once soil is built up to a certain fertility and is not abused, it has a generating ability to maintain and even keep getting better. The root systems go deeper and deeper, bringing up nutrients; the above-ground growth gets bigger and healthier adding more organic material and mulch. As the annual roots and tops decay, they form organic acids that release more minerals from rock formations. After many years of high production, the minerals could be cropped out in certain areas, but applying compost or rock powders could easily maintain the highest fertility. The fertile soil of our once-poor farm has proven the ease of maintaining fertility once you establish it. Our soil is now much darker — almost black — and after heavy rains there is no puddling. When you walk on the wet soil, the crumb structure is so good you barely make tracks. Pests are rarely a problem, and the need for irrigation in dry seasons is much less.

Even though the crops may look their best and production is high, the soil may not yet be perfect. After four years of cover cropping and applying compost, we were growing some of the best looking vegetables you ever saw. We took the vegetables, including carrots, to a natural food store for them to juice. On the second trip in, I was a little disappointed. The manager said our carrots were good, but the California organically grown carrots made a better tasting juice. The next year we again took that same store carrots to juice and the manager reported our carrots were better than last year. The third year we took them carrots, the manager said our carrots were as good as the California carrots. The fourth year we took carrots to the natural food store for juicing, the manager reported our carrots were better than the California carrots — the best he had ever tasted.

This proves that even though a fruit, vegetable or any plant or food crop may look perfect, it could still be lacking. It takes time for all the life in the soil to become active and working in harmony. Healthy soil is more than carbon-nitrogen ratios, moisture, air and minerals. It takes the soil life to really put it in balance. Only when there is balance can the soil feed plants so that optimum taste and health is present.

The results of top fertility are many: no pollution, healthier living, flowing springs, cleaner environment, fewer headaches, less weed problems, no need for pesticides, little need for bagged fertilizer, higher production, peace of mind, and money in the bank. Recycling helps accomplish all of the above.

A Visit to Garden-Ville

Like any production process, success is measured not on the drawing board, but through real-world tests. This static-pile system of composting — letting nature do the work — is tested and proven everyday in the Garden-Ville composting and recycling operations. These pictures will take reader on a behind-the-scenes tour of this large, successful operation.

Garden-Ville's 100-acre site on Interstate 10 east of San Antonio contains a 10-acre pad with a 5-acre retention pond. After allowing for considerable expansion, 50 acres will remain to lease to other recycling companies. The yard is within city limits, next door to the BFI. Garden-Ville and BFI work together on many processes.

This new pad is being readied for composting operations. Fly ash and bottom ash from a local coal-burning power plant are used to build the hard base. The pad is graded to between a 1% and 3% slope, ideal to control runoff, with the entire pad draining into a five-acre retention pond. This sheepfoot roller is used to break up the large, hard chunks of fly ash. The ash products are less expensive than lime, which is also mined in the region, and stick with the recyling theme of the operation.

Old pallets that we collect, up to 10,000 per month, are ground for mulch, for composting, or for fuel for a yet-to-be-installed boiler. They are ground in a tub grinder using two-inch screens on both sides by neighboring BFI and its contract grinding crew. We do not magnet the nails out — they do not hurt the compost or the boiler fuel and in mulches they settle down next to the soil and have yet to cause a problem. Most of the pallets are gum and oak; plastic pallets are removed.

Demolition debris is used the same as the pallets, except we will not take any that could have lead paint on it. Mostly wood, we pick out any metal or asphalt shingles. Some gypsum board is fine, but we usually process it separately.

If you buy or hire a grinder and have a lot of big stumps and logs, use knives or bullet bit teeth such as these. They tear at stumps and logs, breaking them down much faster than hammers. Some grinders have interchangeable hammers or bits.

The big tub grinder owned and operated by BFI. As grinders are designed to destroy things, in the process they self-destruct. The track hoe boasts an opposable "thumb" which allows it to better grasp materials.

Ground-up native tree trimmings — mostly branches pruned from under powerlines — makes an excellent mulch or compost material. It has a closer carbon-nitrogen ratio (more nitrogen) than most other mulches. When it comes from the contractor's chipper/shredder it is usually too big and not uniform. We regrind it using tub grinder with the two-inch screens on both sides.

Cedar trees after being ground in a tub grinder with two-inch screens on both sides; all is sold as mulch. It has an attractive color, decays slowly, superb insulating and mulching abilities, and doesn't attract termites and seems to repel some insects. The large size helps prevent compost piles from collapsing and becoming anaerobic.

A closeup view of native tree trimming materials shown above.

A 110-cubic-yard load of racetrack stable bedding from nearby Retama Park, soaked with urine and manure, is unloaded from a walking floor van.

Static compost piles averaging ten feet in height contain 5,000 to 7,000 cubic yards, with shrinkage from the process start to finished ranging from 38-50%. Each pile is composted for a minimum period of six months and turned at least four times. We have been practicing static pile composting for almost 30 years. We found windrows too wasteful: we could not keep the correct moisture, there is too much exposed surface area, in arid weather they dried out to fast, and in wet weather heavy rains caused them to leach to much. Small windrows also caused a big loss of ammonia nitrogen and carbon dioxide. Not limited to dry areas, our static pile method has also proved successful in areas with 60 inches of annual rainfall.

A tractor turning compost, but very inefficiently. He is running too great a distance. Proper method calls for picking up a full scoop, backing up, turning, and dumping as soon as possible. A cycle should be completed every 35-45 seconds.

In this view the tractor is turning compost but running its front wheels up on the pile compacting the bottom layer which needs air the most. He should run up to the pile but not touch it with the front wheels, dumping the bucket from the highest position.

These old porcelain water-wasting commodes were traded in to the city for a rebate when replaced with newer low-volume models. We can't compost them, but we grind them in a slow-speed grinder with two-inch screen. The resulting product is a beautiful white aggregate ranging from a course sand up to two inches in size that can be screened to any desired size within that range for use as a decorative aggregate.

This Maxigrind does a good job of grinding commodes. We also use it to grind waste candy with materials such as cottonseed hulls used to make cattle feed. The Maxigrind is very versatile, utilizing bullet teeth or knives and running at low speed with high torque. While good for grinding stumps, it was inefficient grinding brush and other waste because it is not continuous. Operators had to wait for the ram to back up before feeding another scoop of material.

A view of the grinding drum in the Maxigrind. We were using the bullet teeth/bits to grind asphalt. It could also be outfitted with hammers.

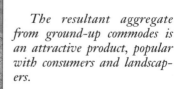

The resultant aggregate from ground-up commodes is an attractive product, popular with consumers and landscapers.

A compost pile under construction. The load of vegetable waste that has just been dumped in front that will be evenly distributed on top of the darker looking material which is pecan hulls that had been dumped one-half cubic yard at a time atop stable bedding. Later, paunch manure and sawdust will be added to each pile in the row of materials in front of the larger master pile. After the desired volume of each ingredient is in the row of piles, they will all be pushed up and added to the master pile. A new master pile is started every six to eight weeks.

High-moisture paunch manure and very-high-moisture vegetables were parked on a 12-inch layer of dry sawdust until we have time to blend them properly while making a new compost pile. The dry sawdust catches and soaks up any liquids that would normally drain away. The liquids are too valuable to waste; the dry sawdust needs it. Then the wet sawdust and high-moisture materials are picked up together and added to the master compost pile.

A loader dumping wet sawdust and paunch manure in front of the master compost pile. After all the other waste materials are dumped, the combination will be pushed up and added to the master pile.

Our one and only try at windrowing — when we were composting for our farm — quickly taught us that windrows were wasteful. Most important, the static-pile compost grew better crops, especially if we applied it early and allowed the composting action to finish in the soil.

We aerate our retention pond by pumping water into the air through 16 homemade sprinklers using gasoline engine-powered four-inch pump. We later changed to 10-horsepower electric power, pumping three times the volume at less cost. This five-acre pond, which accepts the runoff from a ten-acre pad, is designed to handle double the rainfall expected in a 24-hour period during a 100-year rain, giving us ample water for dry spells and fire control. With a shutoff valve to cut the sprinklers, the pressure can be diverted to a four-inch pipeline with numerous valves around the sides of compost pad. The aeration system is simple in the extreme. The homemade system is simply a four-inch main in the center of the pond. Ten-foot lateral branches of two-inch pipe run ten feet to each side. Then six-foot, six-inch vertical stands of one-inch pipe are capped with a PVC cap. Two 1/4-inch holes are drilled opposite each other, angling about 30 degrees and spraying about 18 feet in the air.

This watergun is used to wet piles using water from the retention pond if needed, but mostly to spray waste liquids from tanker trucks that we are paid to dispose. We also use it to control road dust, on material to be ground, or directly onto compost piles depending on the type of liquid.

Wetting a pile with waste brewery liquids directly from a tanker truck equipped with pump and hose.

One of our tractors with an air-cooled engine. Notice the bucket has been enlarged to almost double the capacity which can be safely accomplished as the materials moved weigh about one-half the machine's design load.

This closeup shows our shop-built bucket enlargement.

After numerous problems with factory-built truck beds we decided to build them ourselves. This one has been in continuous service for 16 years without a single problem. We build the hinges, door locking system and all.

The barn-style doors open completely and can be held to the bed sides.

Note the bed of this truck, again home-made, but a later version than pictured at left. Metal beds are one of the biggest mistakes that can be made transporting compost. Everything sticks to rusty steel. Notice how cleanly the material slid out of this wood bed. When hauling manure and moist compost, wood will out perform and outlast metal every time. Lined with common pine, the wood becomes highly polished with use and is practically self-cleaning. It lasts for years.

While dumping, the doors are normally hooked back against the sideboards. The driver unhooks them before the bed is all the way down and then pulls away from the pile before latching them so he won't have to step on freshly dumped material.

This aluminum trailer can haul 60 cubic yards in a load. We installed a teflon liner for safety and longevity. The bed reaches 30 feet in the air while dumping. Uneven dumping could tip it over.

Another portable screen, well-built but of poor design for compost. We use it on small aggregate only.

One of our homemade vibrating screens. It did the job when we didn't have trammels.

Another one of our homemade screens, this one stationary, loads directly into trucks.

Another view of one of the old screens that loads directly into the truck.

One of our screens that is portable. It is well built and trouble free. We frequently rent it out.

Our best portable screen, It gives two sizes and overs and a trailer can be parked under any of the three conveyors.

One of our own design screens that we are screening 1/4 inch. This is the first trammel screen we had built; we still have some improvements to make. For all mesh sizes 1/2 inch and smaller we use stainless wire. Stainless steel screens product much faster then black steel. Larger sizes tend not to clog and the added cost of stainless is not required.

We are putting up five of these custom units, but only one at a time so we can continually add improvements. The later ones will load directly into trucks.

A ten-yard charge hopper is used to feed the screen. It is gated for variable volume feed.

The drums with different size mesh can easily be changed out with a tractor affixed with a homemade boom. The entire changeout takes two men only about 15 minutes.

This boom attaches to the tractor bucket. With the loop of chain, the screen is lifted into place allowing each unit to screen various sizes and type of material.

A closeup view of the stainless steel screen we use for greater production. The wire remains slick and shiny; particularly sticky materials might hang up for a while, but soon break free.

This small screen was put together from junk for under $1,000. We still use it everyday, all day long at the bagging operation. It is slow, but fast enough to keep up with a bagging crew.

One of our six homemade bagging machines allowing us to bag six different products at one time. We can use one operator per machine or three if needed.

If the wind is not blowing too high we can load directly into a customer's low trailer.

To provide a full service to our customers, we also rent compost spreaders. This truck has a chain to move material to rear and double beaters for even spreading. Also has a gate to adjust rate of application.

In a massive effort to recapture nutrients to the soil, sludge from New York is transported by container and then hauled by truck to location where it will be spread in the desert of western Texas.

A bag of composted vivo sludge that we get from the City of Austin, Texas. The city composts its moist sewage sludge mixed with ground-up tree trimmings. Their oversized windows are for all practical purposes static piles. We buy it in bulk, compost it further, re-screen it, and bag it for sale.

An excellent compost spreader being used in west Texas to put out vivo.

The best test of compost is to grow plants. Here, keeping with the recycling theme of our operation, a ring cut from an underground fiberglass fuel tank contains a bed. We also clean them up and sell them to home gardeners.

Old feed tubs also are fine vehicles for testing soil mixes. Letting the plant do the testing is much better than the lab. However we do get some lab testing done.

This old tractor tire with the sidewall cut out also serves as a test garden bed. At any one point in time we have a hundred or more tests underway at Garden-Ville.

A inexpensive, small-mesh wire cage that quickly un-pins to turn or remove the compost. We make them but, the home gardener can easily make his/her own. There is also a 'butterfly wing" compost turner hanging in it. This little tool works good with ground up materials, grass and leaves but it hangs up if you have sticks and branches in the compost. Beside it is a collapsible tomato cage we make from galvanized fence panel.

A three compartment compost bin built by a home gardener. It is important not to forget that the lessons we have learned composting on a grand scale can be easily transferred to smaller operations.

Large-Scale Composting

I got into the compost business by accident. I made my living working on the railroad. Our farm was more of a hobby than a necessity, although it was a good place to live and raise our family. Besides the usual farm crops and animals, we raised vegetables, up to twenty acres some years, and did it all organically. Our fertilizer was lots of manure gathered from our and the neighbor's cow pens. We always kept a few big piles around.

A visiting friend who was a landscaper spied our manure piles and pestered me until I finally sold him some. We loaded it by hand using manure forks. He paid me forty dollars for four yards. I got to looking at that money and thought, Gosh, that was much easier than spreading that manure in the field and plowing, disking, planting, cultivating, irrigating, harvesting, then going to market and letting someone else dictate the price. Then the thought struck. Why don't I sell compost?

But I soon learned that at that time, few people, including farmers, knew what compost was. Next, the landscaper's mother wanted some compost mixed with sand, then his uncle wanted compost mixed with sand and topsoil. Soon word got out that I had manure mixed with sand and/or soil, and here came the landscapers. I was forced into the soil mixing business. It wasn't long before I used up all the rotted manure. Then I had to use manure that was still raw to make the mixes. I explained to customers, "This stuff may be a little hot," but they bought it anyway. One day I made a delivery to a woman who operated a small nursery. She grew shrubs in big containers and I noticed her containers were free of weeds, while other nurseries always had a weed problem. I complimented her on the good job she did weeding, and she replied, "Malcolm your soil/compost mix never has any weeds in it."

Soon word got out that Beck had a weed-free soil, sand, and manure mix. Then I had to buy more trucks and tractors.

BEGINNERS ADVICE: KEEP IT SIMPLE

Every living thing will sooner or later die. When it dies, it is going to rot whether you want it to or not. Composting is the *art* of working with the decay process in an *economical* way. If you are thinking of setting up a large composting operation, you need to determine the best ways of making sure your product is good and your operation set up in a profitable way.

Trucking will be your greatest expense. You can minimize those costs by using all the organic materials available in your immediate area. Find out what resources there are nearby. Is there a feedlot? Are there horse stables? Is a food-processing plant in your area? You can make compost with all manure or almost no manure. Take a close look at the prairie or the forest floor. You will learn Nature uses very little manure to help compost all the carbon materials she deposits there each year. You will never get in trouble composting or using a high carbon ratio compost. High-percentage manure composting requires a little more art.

Study Nature to master the art. Study the books to understand the sciences.

REGULATIONS

The regulatory agencies — the EPA, the water commission, or the health department in your area — will probably have rules about what you can and cannot do. Most of them will be sensible and have a good reason behind them. Some will appear stupid (and may be), but you will have to abide by them. Don't fight the agencies; they can make your life miserable. Instead, become friends with them. They can be a big help to you, and usually will be. Many times over the years, the water commission, air quality people, or the aquifer water authorities were out inspecting, visiting or following up on a complaint at my compost operation. I always answered all their questions honestly and showed them more than they asked to see. I would give them a full tour. A lot of the time I would ask them for advice. A suggestion from one agent saved me more than eight thousand dollars in taxes in one year alone.

Dealing with agents was usually pleasant. Once a new neighbor moved into the area. Even though she was a mile away, she got a whiff of some turkey manure being unloaded one evening. As soon as we opened the doors the next morning, an air quality agent was out quoting me the rules I was violating and the fines I would receive. This guy was new in the department, and he was really going to throw the book at me. I calmly invited him for a tour so we could find the problem. I explained our composting methods and all the materials we saved from the landfills. After about thirty-five minutes of answering his questions (he seemed very interested), I took him back to where I figured the smell originated. I explained that the load had to sit in the truck in the heat a long time. Because of mechanical problems, the truck couldn't be unloaded. As a result, the manure did stink when we finally got the truck working. He said, "Mr. Beck, I don't smell anything." I said, "Yeah, but it really stunk when we unloaded it." He repeated in a louder voice, "Mr. Beck, I do not smell anything," so I dropped the subject and started driving back to the office. The agent remained quiet for some time before he spoke. Then he said, "You know I do have to write this up." I immediately thought, "Uh-oh, he is going to get me now." When he spoke again his words were real comforting. He said, "The way I am going to approach this is, with the standard of living we have today, all of us create a lot of waste and that waste has to be recycled, and it is not feasible to haul it great distances to do the recycling. As a result, we all have to learn to put up with some of the unpleasantness of the recycling process." Boy, did I ever agree with his approach. I haven't heard from him since. And my respect for the authorities is holding strong.

SELECTING A LOCATION

Perception is reality. Try to find an out-of-sight location. People smell with their eyes and on suggestion. I spoke with a fellow who operated a compost yard for a small town. He said when they announced in their daily paper a compost operation was proposed at that location, the very next day they were getting odor complaints from that area.

Nobody wants to smell or look at someone else's waste. When people put out their garbage they just want it to go away. Their reply is usually, "Not In My Backyard!" There is no way that can happen. Anywhere you go you will be in some-one's backyard.

Way out in the desert of West Texas, miles and miles from the closest neighbor, there was a court battle when a company wanted to dump a thin layer of sludge over soil that desperate-ly needed it. It is the same anywhere you go. I visited with the sewer plant engineer of a little town up in Canada. He told me they were composting their processed sludge with yard trim-mings and selling it to the citizens at a fair profit. But the town was out-growing their little five-acre yard. They bought some acreage a few miles out of town where they planned to expand. Before they could get started, the neighbors, although none were really close, were screaming "Not In My Backyard!" They decided to move the plant out another five miles and ran into the same thing. They kept going out and out until they were fifty miles from town and still met stiff opposition. The last I heard, they still had not found a location that wasn't in someone's backyard.

I know a private composter up in the state of Washington that has a compost yard in the middle of a town with homes, apartments and businesses all around him. He does an excel-lent job of composting, and foul odors are rare even though he is composting sludge and tree trimmings. Still, when a new neighbor moves nearby, there is usually an odor complaint as soon as the new people discover what he is doing. He told me that some people smell better with their eyes than their noses. On my first visit to that compost yard, the owner/operator was not there, so I decided to place a call to the regulatory agency in his area.

When the agent came to the phone, I asked him if he was aware of that compost operation in the middle of town, and he quickly replied "Yes, I have been watching him, and I am getting ready to shut him down," then he hung up. I mentioned this to the operator and he got a big laugh. He told me the agent was his biggest supporter and had gotten so tired of explaining and even arguing with some citizens that he quickly cuts them off with an answer that most of them want to hear.

Cities and towns will probably set up compost operations near their landfills; the zoning is correct and neighbors should tolerate it. Private composters will have to search far and wide for a site because of the NIMBY syndrome. Start looking near your raw material supply; you may be more readily accepted there. At least try to find a location between supply and where the product will be sold because of the tremendous cost of trucking. Also try to situate downwind if there are or will be neighbors.

SITE DEVELOPMENT

After the location is acquired, design for ease of operation and flow of traffic around the yard. Studying and speaking with operators of other compost yards helps tremendously.

The pad is extremely important. My first compost yard has been my only real problem. It was not graded with the proper slope of 1 to 2%. We put down six inches of hard limestone base, but the soil under it was not stabilized. If I had removed the topsoil, it would have been much better. After a few years of heavy truck and tractor traffic, the limestone started sinking in areas and rising in others. Soon I had large puddles of water after rains, which we had to soak up with scarce dry sawdust or pump out. Also the uneven surface made it hard to operate loaders. They were either digging into the pad and getting limestone rock in the compost being loaded or leaving too much material remaining on the surface. This is a constant problem, and hard to correct once the operation is in business, because it would mean shutting down for a while. Do it right to start with. Highway engineers who build roads in your area can the best give advice on how to stabilize the soil at your location.

Plant lots of big evergreen trees around the site. Trees stop noise and dust, trap blowing trash, slow the wind, and hide the operation. They also give your yard a landscaped look and stop people from smelling with their eyes.

My newest compost pad was built by a road construction company. They stabilized the soil using lime at the rate of 6% thoroughly mixed in ten inches deep, then we topped that with three inches of fly ash, a by-product from a coal-burning power plant. The fly ash was watered and rolled the same as you would treat limestone. At first I was worried that it wasn't setting up hard like limestone, but with time it finally did. So far the fly ash is holding up well. It was a big savings over limestone or any other surface I could have used, besides it is a recycled product that goes with the theme of our new research and recycling park.

The statement from the young air quality agent that checked on my smelly turkey manure was so correct. With our standard of living we all *do* create a lot of waste. We can't make it disappear. It has to be recycled, and at a location near where it is created. The recycling has to be simple and economical and at times there will be unpleasantness of noise, odors, traffic and dust. Most people will live a safe distant from the nuisance of their waste being recycled. However, those near enough to experience any unpleasantness should somehow be compensated. I would think cutting property taxes to the degree of nuisances being tolerated would be a fair way. And the citizens who don't have it in their backyard could pick up the difference. Even if science did some day discover a way to just make what we consider waste disappear, Nature would still demand that we recycle for our very survival.

GETTING STARTED

Always start with a good supply of dry carbon materials. Carbons can be stockpiled, but wet nitrogen material can't because it will smell bad and draw flies. Start the pile using two parts carbon to one part nitrogen and see how it works. From there, you may make changes — either more carbon or more nitrogen. If the pile doesn't heat but smells and draws flies, you have too much nitrogen. Add more carbon. If it heats and doesn't smell but works too slowly, you may want to add more nitrogen. Either way you need to keep experimenting until you get the feel for the right proportions. Remember, composting is an art, and like any art it can only be mastered with practice.

I believe in keeping it simple, efficient and economical. Try static piles before using windrow turners or some expensive in-vessel methods. It is best to study Nature. Do what she has been efficiently doing since the beginning. The static pile is very efficient. Very little moisture is wasted.

We make our piles 10 to 12 ft. high. They can soak up our annual rainfall of 29 inches without any leaching out the bottom. We turn the piles usually after big rains; it re-heats and drives off any excess moisture, making it ready for the next rain. We seldom have to water our compost piles. The large size retains the moisture that comes in the material being composted, so we don't even have to water when the pile is first made. If your materials are dry to start with, you must wet them while they are being ground or mixed. You cannot thoroughly wet a really dry pile from the top. It has no capillary attraction, and the water will run straight down and puddle on the ground.

EQUIPMENT NEEDED

In the early '70s, when I decided to make compost for sale, someone told me you needed to make windrows. I tried windrows, but it didn't take me long to learn that all I was doing was drying the material out. Once it was dry, it was almost impossible to get uniform moisture in it again. Building static piles and turning them only four times has been my composting method ever since. The secret to static composting is to be sure to keep the carbon a little on the high side. I have never tested, but I believe it is around 30 or 35 to 1, or possibly higher. The next most important thing is to make sure the pile is fluffy and not packed down.

An operator from Kentucky visited me one time and said static piles would not work where he lived, although he admitted he had not tried them. He was using forced-air windrows. Two years later I was in his neighborhood. I stopped in for a visit and noticed he had abandoned his forced air and changed to my method. He said the static piles were much more efficient than his old way. I have never seen or heard of static pile composting failing, but I have visited or consulted with numerous windrow operations that failed or were failing or could be doing better with static piles. In almost every case, the operators were not able to keep adequate moisture in the windrows. I know of one operator in East Texas where the annual rainfall is around 60 inches. He composts yard trimmings. He started with windrows but has now changed to the static pile method.

I am not ruling out windrow turning machines. They do a good job of blending and drying out materials that are too wet. I even intend to buy one someday to dry out materials so they will screen faster during wet seasons. They would also help dry materials down so we can get greater volumes on the big trucks without overloading when we ship long distances. Another place windrow turners come in handy is around some feedlots where the manure is so caked-up in big, hard chunks that it has to be broken up. They might also be helpful in some of those areas where there usually isn't bulking carbon material around to raise the carbon-nitrogen ratio and fluff up the pile.

Keep it simple. Don't let salesmen talk you into buying equipment you do not need. I see this happen way too often. Visit compost operations similar to what yours will be, using the same feedstock, in the same environment, annual rainfall, evaporation, etc. Find those that have been in operation for a few years. Learn from their mistakes, They usually like to talk about them anyway.

Two gentlemen came to me once and said they had some money saved and asked if I would get mad if they went into the composting business in a location near one of my distant outlets. I said I would not only not get mad, but I would even purchase all their finished compost for that outlet which was 70 miles away. I could save transportation costs. I invited them to see exactly how I was making my compost. They would be using the same raw products I used in almost the exact same environment — no way could they foul up. I suggested the type and size of equipment they would need and even helped them secure a lease on some property near their raw material supply and assured the landowner and neighbors there wouldn't be any odor or fly problems.

Months went by and I hadn't heard from my new friends. Finally a call arrived. Could I come up? They were having some problems. On the drive up I was wondering what kind of problems they could be having. My instructions to them were so simple. All they had to do was to put the stable bedding — which already had a perfect carbon-nitrogen ratio of wood shavings, hay and manure — into a big pile. It already had enough moisture to get the composting action started. It was fluffy enough to get oxygen and never go anaerobic. And they already had a loader to turn the pile after each rain.

Upon arriving I found a disaster. The flies were unbearable. I have never seen flies so bad anywhere in my life, and I didn't see any big compost piles. The had bought wrong equipment and were doing just the opposite of what I told them. Instead of static piles that would conserve moisture, they made small windrows which quickly lost the little moisture in the stable bedding from the urine and manure. They didn't pick the glass bottles and other trash out. The windrow turner broke it up into little pieces, so now they couldn't screen it out. They then had to pipe in water from a distance at a big expense. They had purchased leaky pipe to try to wet the small windrows, but the material was so dry it was hydrophobic (resisted wetting). The water just ran straight down through the windrows to the soil and created the perfect environment to grow fly larva.

I asked them why they tried another method to compost other than my proven way. They said they bought some compost science books and wanted to make a better product in less time. Had these two gentlemen not bought the books or at least not tried to apply the science until after they learned to make compost, they would be in business today.

GRINDERS

If you have tree trimmings to grind, check into hiring the grinding done. There are many grinders around that need extra work to keep the machine and crew busy. Grinders are designed to destroy things and, in the process, they are continually self-destructing. You will quickly discover they are expensive to operate. If you decide you need one on-site for daily grinding, again talk to someone who has owned and operated one for a year or longer. Most popular brands are advertised in magazines like *Biocycle*. You can call the dealers, and they will direct you to long-time owners and operators.

I have owned three different kinds of grinders. One they quit making. The second was a good machine, the manufacturer stood behind it well, but it was too small. The third was a good machine that I really liked, but I can't recommend it. Neither the factory nor the dealer would back it up when there were problems. If you have large branches and tree stumps to grind, get one that has bullet bit teeth or knives to do the grinding. They are much more efficient on big stumps of eight-inch diameter and larger. You can't grind big logs by beating on them with hammers. We use two-inch screens in the grinders for making mulch and composting. The product comes out three inches to fines. The finer particles compost fast; the larger particles keep the static compost pile fluffy and well aerated so less turning is required. After compost is completed, the large material can be separated with a screen, and you then not only have compost but all size materials to be used for lawn dressing, bed preparation and a dark, partly decomposed mulch that is excellent and feeds the plant while mulching.

POWER SOURCES

Use three-phase electricity on all stationary equipment such as small grinders, screens and conveyors. High-voltage electricity is the most efficient, trouble-free power source there is. The next best choice is equipment with air-cooled diesel engines. Even some of our tractors have Deutz air-cooled engines; they are very fuel efficient and dependable. We started with coolant-cooled engines and spent too much time blowing the radiators free of trash. Air-cooled engines eliminate 40% of maintenance problems. We demand them on all new equipment that's used around blowing leaves, grass, shavings, etc.

LOADERS

All-wheel drive, articulated loaders are the only way to go. Small, rear-wheel drive tractors, such as used on backhoes, are useless for loading. The front wheels where the load is are too small. With the load on the front, the weight is raised off the rear wheels, causing them to lose traction. But it is nice to have one of these tractors on the property with a box scraper or weed and brush shredder to use as the need arises. Start with a small loader if finances and needs are low. Purchase a larger — 3 to 6 cubic yards — loader when needed but keep the small loader. It will come in handy to load small trucks. It is always good to have a second loader in case one breaks down.

If your loaders are only to be used in composting, you can enlarge the buckets since the compost material will weigh half or less as much as the dirt, sand or rock they were designed to handle. We add four to six inches to the cutting edge and six to ten inches to the sides and top. This increases the volume by 30 to 50%, enabling that much extra work to be accomplished each day.

COMPOST TURNERS

We use large, 6 cubic yard tractors and only turn four to five times, depending how fast we will need the compost. It takes about six to eight months from start to finish. A good operator can easily make about 80 cycles (pick up, turn and dump) per hour at six yards per scoop. That comes to 480 cubic yards per hour and costs about ten cents to turn a cubic yard. The loaders used for turning have good resale value and many other uses around a compost yard. They also have a lot less down-time than a windrow turner. If the material to be composted is full of bottles, Styrofoam cups, and other trash, it will have to be picked over first if you are using windrow turners. They will break everything up into small pieces that can't be screened out. Turning with loaders won't break up trash, and it can easily be screened out of the finished compost

SCREENS

During my first seven years in business, I didn't use or own a screen. The day I finally got a screen, the demand for our products doubled and we soon doubled our selling price. Screened material looks good; unscreened materials may be of same quality, but it looks trashy. Screens do more for quality appearance and sales than any piece of equipment or salesman you could employ. It costs very little to screen materials. We kept records one month and the electric bill was less than 1/2 cent per cubic yard. We convey the screened material directly into the trucks, which we found to be another savings. Some of our trucks are too high for tractor loading and would require loading ramps. When trucks are continually loaded from the side with loaders, they soon get banged up and start looking shabby and cheap. Screening materials directly into the trucks before each delivery has other advantages.

Leaving screened materials in stockpiles too long has caused problems. It tends to lump together, trucks and tractors run over the edges and pack it, or it gets contaminated with other materials while later being loaded. However, some materials screen too slowly to have trucks waiting, and you will have to do some stockpiling. We now have eight screens, three of them are trammels and the rest are vibrating.

Why so many screens you may wonder? We need them. We screen different products to different sizes, and we operate three different locations. We don't want trucks waiting for a screen. All of our screens were purchased used. Some we had to redesign, others we repaired, and some we built with mostly used materials. However, we have four screens on order — all trammel with stainless steel screening mesh. We make all kinds of mixes, including some with a high percentage of clay, which tends to stick to the wire. We learned that rusty wire holds product to it. Stainless steel is always slick and shiny, product sticks for a while, builds up to a point, then breaks free exposing slick wire. As needed we are replacing all of the screens with stainless steel. In some cases efficiency was increased as much as 300%. With some products, however, it didn't make much difference.

I visited a compost operation that was just getting started in a big city. The operator had already purchased a monster-sized screen that cost well over $200,000. I considered it a poor design. I hope the operator had a good plan and it was not another case of letting a salesman design his operation. All eight of our existing screens didn't cost nearly that much. The four trammel screens we have on order are my design and are being built in a friend's welding shop. When they are completed and in operation the cost will be about $36,000 each.

QUALITY CONTROL

Perception is reality. A clean, screened product, free of rocks, roots, seeds and trash is your best sales tool. As mentioned earlier, once we started screening our sales doubled. Many times after delivering to a home owner, a neighbor would see the screened compost or soil mix and order a load. We often sold three or four people on the same street. Looks will make the first sale, but it takes performance for repeat orders. Success in the garden or an extra-green lawn holds customers forever. Burn up the lawn or kill some plants, and the customers are gone forever. I had a driver load from the wrong pile once and deliver material that was very raw and still smelling. It was a long time before I sold that customer or his neighbors compost again.

LAB TESTS

Before you waste time and money on laboratory testing, give the product the plant test. Plant seeds and transplants in it. If they grow well, the compost is OK. If they do not do well, then you can get a lab test. Find a recommended lab. Introduce yourself to them and let them know what you are composting and how. And then stay with the same lab. You can't make adjustments on analysis from two different labs. After you make adjustments, go back to plant testing.

We do a lot of testing by growing. We plant a lot of trees, shrubs, vegetables and flowers. When the test is completed, we use what we can and usually give the rest away to employees, customers and neighbors. It spreads the word about compost and creates a lot of good will. We gain more by giving the plants away than if we sold them. The cost was already written off as research anyway.

Do *not* have an institution research your products. I did that once, and they destroyed the reputation of that product forever — even after extensive testing that proved them wrong. In order to show they are experts, most institutions will have something good *and* bad to say about a product unless there is a sizable research grant attached. If a university professor publishes something good or bad, be it true or false, it becomes law.

A SIMPLE COMPOST TEST

To tell if compost is ready, I roll up the sleeve on my right arm and dig my hand into the compost pile up to my elbow and pull some out and smell. If it has a bad odor, other than ammonia, it is not ready. All of the proteins are not yet digested. If you can only detect an ammonia smell, it might be ready. To tell for sure, wash your hand and go to the office or someplace away from the pile and have someone smell both hands. Women who don't smoke have the sharpest noses. If both hands smell the same, the compost is ready for most uses. Caution: if you stick your hand into a rank pile, the lingering smell is almost impossible to wash off. I use tomato juice or salt water. Rub your hands with either until the smell is gone. Even if the compost passes the smell test, you may still need to let it cure for a while if it is going to be used to sprout seeds or in potting mixes. For flower bed preparation, mulching, and spreading on lawns it is ready to use. Let the curing action continue in or on the soil. That is where Nature usually does it anyway.

COMPOSTING PROBLEMS & SOLUTIONS
Smells

Odor has no respect for boundaries. The best fence can't hold it; it even escapes while you are watching. Once it is loose, you can't catch it or put it back. It generously divides itself among all your downwind neighbors. The only way to control odors is to anticipate and try to prevent them. I have had a few escapes that attracted unwanted attention. I mentioned the turkey manure earlier. It was the only incident that brought out the air quality people. It was also the shortest of duration and the least foul, but it just happened to go in the wrong direction.

The worst odor I created was when I was composting whole onions. I was getting forty cubic yards per day, six days per week, and I was running out of room and also dry sawdust to blend with them. I was backing off on the carbon to save space and also using some wet sawdust. There was no smell until we started the first turning. Wow — was that booger strong! We did finally get it turned by waiting for the correct wind direction.

Whole vegetables are the hardest to compost, even meat products are easier. Vegetables rot from the inside out. They go anaerobic on the inside, but the liquids are not released to be absorbed by the dry carbon until everything is good and stinky because the cell walls break down so slowly. We learned to grind the vegetables first or to grind them with a carbon bulking product. Ground up, the liquids started releasing much sooner and a little at a time so oxygen could enter. We could compost them whole if we used double the amount of dry-bulking carbon and waited much longer before the first turning. There wouldn't be a bad odor, but it took up needed space and time.

Flies

If you compost high-protein materials, vegetable waste or manure, you will have a fly problem in the beginning. We did at all three of our locations. At the first location, the problem lasted almost three years. I didn't know any better and tried to control flies with non-toxic sprays or poisons in bait traps. This approach just seemed to aggravate the problem. I finally decided to just live with them because I didn't want to use toxic materials around the compost. Organic growers didn't like it, and besides, it was costing too much for the little good it did. When I stopped using the sprays the flies started getting fewer and fewer. Their natural enemies such as dragonflies, robber flies and other predators and parasites started moving in. The problem improved, but the flies weren't controlled as well as I wished until fly parasites became commercially available. I released them around our compost sites for a while, then I decided to go to the main source. I began releasing predators at the stables and other places the manure came from. The operators of these locations soon learned how well the parasites work and now release on their own.

The parasites deposit their eggs in the late stage of the fly larva or early pupa stage. When some of them arrive in our yard along with the manure, the parasites hatch here and the fly larva and pupae die. Now we seldom need to purchase and release parasites.

At our newest and largest compost yard it took less than three months to get the fly problem well under control. We started immediately with the parasites at our location and the new places we got the manure from. The parasites alone couldn't do the job completely until help came from the dragonflies and swallows that came out in droves every evening after they discovered the good hunting around our piles and the retention pond offering water to go with their meal of flies.

A few flies around a compost operation are necessary. You shouldn't, even if you could, eliminate them completely. A few flies keep their natural enemies coming around and the ecology stays in balance, and also the flies keep the compost piles well inoculated with numerous species of the necessary decomposing microbes they are able to carry from place to place.

Marketing & Sales

When I first started commercial composting, all of my promotional effort was directed toward the agriculture community. I got nowhere. I was forced to market to the city consumer. It turned out to be a good thing. Those city customers are learning more about compost and how it builds the soil. They are beginning to make demands of elected officials and with voting dollars.

I have found that having a good, reliable product is the most important marketing tool you can have. Much of my business has grown by word-of-mouth. Satisfied customers tell others and eventually the word spreads that you have the best compost and soils around.

Another important thing I have done to increase sales is to educate people about the importance of compost. This doesn't always make a sale right away, but unless people understand how important it is to recycle waste and feed the soil, our business efforts will all be futile. So I talk to people whenever I can and explain how compost works. I never discourage people from making their own compost, because usually once someone gets used to having good compost in the garden, they will never be able to make enough at home. The result is more sales.

Let people know you are there and have a consistently good product, and the sales will follow. Being honest with your customers, respecting their needs and opinions, and treating everyone right will help your business grow as well. Don't get too greedy to start with. Businesses are like plants — they need time to grow and produce. Read and think over the seven laws for success listed in the end of this book.

You can develop your place in the market by listening and talking with the people around you. Look at special markets that may be in your area. Are there retirement homes where the people can afford good gardens but may not be able to do all the work? Are there new developments where young people have lots of energy but less money? Is the soil in your area lacking in a specific nutrient? Find out what is going on around you and fill the gaps. Your business will grow.

And never forget the agricultural community. The lawns and gardens of the metroplex can use compost, but our food-producing soils are our security for the future.

VALUE-PRICE

To Nature, compost is extremely valuable. Returning organic material back to the soil is a must if quality of life is to continue. However, we — as supposedly intelligent creatures — have continually devalued compost, first by saying we need to compost the organics because they are filling up our limited landfill space too fast. More value was put on the hole in the ground than on the food the soil dearly needed. Then after a few cities learned to save landfill space by composting, they devalued it still further by giving it away or selling it too cheap. Anything free or sold for very little is given just that value — very little. With the very low value put on compost, private composters have little interest, which drops a still greater burden on the cities and their valuable holes.

We sell compost at $25.00 per cubic yard, and so far the city of San Antonio has not devalued compost by giving it away or selling it too cheap. The city is making compost and they are intelligent enough to use it on their own properties. The city of Austin also makes compost. They call their product Dillo Dirt. They use some but most is sold. However, they have an excellent program. They sell through distributors only. There is no limit to the number of distributors, but distributorships cost a couple of hundred dollars per year which limits it to the serious. The distributors do the promotion and advertise the value and set the price accordingly. As demand goes up the city goes up on the per-yard price to the distributors.

Cities should use as much of their compost on their own properties as possible, usually they will not have enough. It sets a good example to citizens. The citizens equally share in the value of water, fertilizer and pesticide savings. And tax money is not used to compete with private enterprise. This practice also encourages the private composting and mulching industry — another good thing for the economy of the community.

DIVERSIFY FOR MORE SALES

Special soil blends sounded like a good idea, so I started mixing. I always played in the dirt as a kid anyway. I came up with what I thought were some good blends and sold a few. The people who bought them always had some complaint and their growing problems were blamed on the mix. I finally wised up and let them design their own. Some were almost the same as mine, some not as good. But if they designed the mix they would make it work and I didn't get any blame. After a while, I would make suggestions for improvement, which most accepted.

Whenever someone, especially a landscaper, ends up with a good mix we put his name on it. That, of course, made him proud, and soon he was bragging to other people, which sure didn't hurt our sales any. We now encourage people to blend their own soil mixes. When a mix turns out to be good, we usually keep it in stock.

Besides the compost and weed-free, composted topsoil, we keep four different types of sand, several different types and sizes of mulch, peat, perlite, vermiculite, charcoal, minerals and fertilizers in stock for experimenters to choose from. We now have potting soil, landscape soil, garden soil, azalea soil, four-way mix, and some others.

Our most famous soil mix is the Eddy Garcia Rose Mix. A real likable fellow came in my office one day and said he was a member of the rose society. He grew roses but had never won a trophy or even a ribbon. He wanted my suggestions on soil because he figured that was his problem. I knew nothing about roses so I suggested he talk to some successful growers to get some ideas and then come back to do some blending from all of our materials. Eddie showed up about four or five Saturdays in a row with his wheelbarrow and shovel. My store manager suggested I ask him to leave if he wasn't going to buy something because he was in the way of trucks loading and unloading. I had already grown to like the fellow, so I couldn't ask him to leave. I said, "Eddie, if you come up with a good mix please let me know." Later that evening, Eddie said he had finally come up with something he liked and asked us to mix and deliver twelve cubic yards to his home.

It was several months before I heard from Eddie again. When he finally called he was so ecstatic he could hardly talk. He had won 20 trophies and ribbons! By the end of the year, Eddie had won a trophy case full. In April of 1983, the American Rose Society came to San Antonio with their national show. The show offered the Nicholson Bowl, the highest award offered in the United States, which required nine perfect tea roses, each a different species, to win. Eddie Garcia won the $25,000 trophy. Am I glad I didn't ask that guy to leave! That mix is now the standard for all rose growers. It is also used for growing many other plants and trees.

Our potting soil was another mix that didn't come easy. In the early 1970s, I decided I wanted a very good — if not the best — potting soil around. I went to twenty-two different growers that I considered knowledgeable and got twenty-two different blends. I later discussed this with Dr. Parsons, a very knowledgeable horticulturist, and he told me that if I could please 51% of the people, I would have a good product. So I went to Mr. Fanick of Fanick's Nursery, the oldest and most respected grower in San Antonio. I used his suggestions, made a mix and, with his blessing, put his name on it. The one thing I have learned about potting soil is that a high percentage of compost is good, but the compost must be well cured.

YARD TRIMMINGS
Grass Clippings

If you take grass clippings, don't accept bagged clippings if you can help it. If you must, have the person bringing them or an employee dump them immediately for two reasons. We have found a lot of trash in bags that could hurt the quality of the finished product. Make the person who brought it pick it out or take it back so next time he will know better. The second reason is that grass or any green waste becomes anaerobic with a terrible smell in a very short time if left in a plastic bag.

Grass clippings should be left on the lawn. There is no need to pick them up. With mulching mowers the clippings are so small they quickly filter down into the thatch and decompose (compost) in a hurry. The important thing is to mow often for two reasons: it is less shock to the lawn when only a small amount of grass blade is cut each time and a smaller amount of clippings are deposited each mowing. Leaves falling on the lawn can also be shredded in place by mulching mowers. In cooler climates where decomposition is slower, extra nitrogen may need to be added in the spring to keep too much undigested thatch from building up.

If grass clippings are collected, they should be blended with dry carbon bulking material such as brush chips as soon as possible. Green clippings mat together and go anaerobic in a hurry and smell worse than any manure. Green grass can be a bonus to a composting operation if kept free of garbage and handled promptly. Green grass adds needed moisture and nitrogen to the wood chips or any dry carbon material being composted.

Blends of brush chips with a small amount of grass and leaves can easily be composted in static piles with few turnings; we have been doing it for years. Ground-up brush with a small amount of grass and leaves make an excellent mulch; this is mimicking Nature. Why waste the energy composting this material before using? In Nature it all falls mixed together on the forest floor where it composts while it is mulching. We call this mixture *native mulch*.

Mulch

I did a test comparing native mulch with pine bark, taking a cubic yard of each and spreading it four inches thick with about four feet of space between them. I then soaked them with a sprinkler. It rained two days later, and then we had no rainfall at my farm for 113 days. This gave me a good opportunity to see how well the mulch held moisture. This test was started early in the summer, and once a week I took a reading using a good moisture meter. After two weeks, the soil between the two mulched spots registered dry, while the reading through either mulch read wet. For sixty days the needle in the mulched area maxed out on the wet side of the dial before it started moving toward the moist reading. The last reading I took before it rained, ending the test, was on the 105th day. The needle on the meter was in the center range reading moist. I dug through either mulch material and the soil was nice and moist. One afternoon during that test the ambient temperature was 104 degrees. I stuck a thermometer into bare soil near the two mulched areas; the temperature was 120 degrees. The reading through either mulch that day was only 85 degrees — 35 degrees difference. All of the readings were taken a little over one inch deep. On days when the high ambient temperature was in the 90s, the soil under the mulch was in the low 80s. Beneficial soil life and plant roots can't survive in 120-degree dry soil; they prefer 82 degrees with ample moisture.

I did a lot of testing around plants using both the native mulch and hardwood bark. The two were equal in regulating moisture and temperature, but when tested around plants the native mulch was found to be superior. The carbon-nitrogen ratio of the native is much closer to the ratio in rich compost — around 35 or 40 to one. The native blend feeds the plants being mulched, while bark with a carbon-nitrogen ratio of 200 and up causes nutrients to be robbed from the plants being mulched. Pine bark will not stay on a slope, it always slides, blows or washes off. The native mulch clings together and stays in place on steep slopes. The barks are shipped into our San Antonio area from an average distance of three hundred miles, adding a lot of freight cost, and the trucks are polluting the environment the whole distance. The native mulch has very little freight involved. Earthworms love the native mulch; very seldom are earthworms found under the nutrient-weak bark. The native mulch also looks more natural to our San Antonio environment.

SLUDGE COMPOST

Of all the types of compost I have used over the years — on the farm, orchard, vineyard, garden or in containers — sludge works as well or better as any and lasts the longest. Sludge from a sewer plant that has little or no heavy metals and which has been properly composted with yard trimmings is the very best fertilizer/soil conditioner there is.

The higher in the food chain you go, the more nutritious and complex the protein molecule. In the human body, the protein molecule is a very complex molecule that can only be made to dissolve in water under high heat and pressure applied at the same time. This protein is found in sludge. Because the molecule is so complex, it takes the microbes involved in decomposition a while to break it down. The result is that sludge composts more slowly than other kinds of organic waste, but the benefit is that once the microbes break into the molecule, they can feed for a very long time. The result is a very rich substance which maintains its nutrient value for a long time.

I found out some of this when I tried to make pellets out of composted sludge. I ran the material through my pelletizing die that I use for regular fertilizer. The results were great — small, firm pellets that could easily run through a fertilizer spreader. I had visions of dollars dancing in my head. We bagged up some of the material and set it aside for a few days. The next time I walked by the bags I smelled a horrible odor. I couldn't imagine what was going on. On a closer look I found that the bags were moist and full of mold — and really awful smells. To find out what had gone wrong, I checked with a chemist friend. He explained that in the process of pelletizing the sludge, I had applied heat and pressure at the same time. The result was a water-soluble material just perfect for microbes to start working on. My visions of dollars dimmed, but I was impressed by the activity going on in the bags.

Sludge contains the widest type of decomposing microbes found anywhere. Activated sludge is an excellent inoculant to start a compost pile. Two parts carbon from ground pallets, bark, sawdust, or other source to one part sludge works well. If yard trimmings with lots of smaller branches with leaves and buds or any green waste with a closer carbon-nitrogen ratio is used, you may need three or even four parts carbon material to one part sludge. All the sludge I have composted was 60% moisture or less, and static piles worked well. Sludge with higher water content in humid conditions, however, may need to be composted in windrows, at least for a while. Composting sludge along with a lot of yard trimmings and other carbon materials dilutes any heavy metals it may contain down to a safe level. Some metals will even escape as harmless gases.

Sludge composted properly and long enough in good heating piles will be completely free of any dangerous pathogens. The EPA testing required should always be done, not only for safety, but it will allow your product to be used anywhere, anytime and in any amount, even on food crops. The testing will also ease people's minds and help sell the finished product. Sludge should be considered one of our greatest natural resources and should never be wasted.

In the fall of 1995 I had the pleasure of taking a trip with Mr. Charles Walters (founder and publisher of *Acres U.S.A.*, an eco-agricultural monthly publication) to the desert community of Sierra Blanca in West Texas. There is an experiment going on there where they are spreading that sludge made in New York City. Since 1992, they have been spreading trainloads of New York sludge. The spreading is being done scientifically with excellent records being kept. Chuck and I had the opportunity to be taken around by the ranch foreman. After a full day of inspecting and questioning, our curiosity was satisfied. We, and the many research institutions studying that environment affected, could find no negatives.

We found that the sludge is turning the desert into an oasis. The antelope and other wild animals are moving in and prefer to feed in the sludged areas. The native grass is much thicker; in many places it has thickened into a solid cover. Tests have shown that the soil temperature has gone down 15 degrees, lowering the evaporation rate. All of the other many, many benefits of spreading compost are taking place in that desert.

Chuck Walters liked what he saw so well he suggested the sludge should have a better name. People relate sludge to something awful like the scum at the bottom of a waste oil barrel. Even the word biosolids was too closely kin to the word sludge. We needed a better name. Because of the life it was bringing to the desert, he suggested we rename it *vivo*, a word that means *life*.

After they told us of the mountains of record keeping they had to do, Chuck and I had the same thought — typical bureaucracy. Still, good records need to be kept so there is never any doubt of the benefits *vivo* does when returned to the land. Maybe with the availability of *vivo*, and it's proven safety, we can take the money normally paid to landfill it and direct that savings to making a less costly compost that all farmers can afford.

Vivo (sludge) is the premier fertilizer and all should go back to farm acres. Instead, most of it today is being wasted in landfills. Properly composting sludge with enough carbon materials can dilute the heavy metals to a very safe level, and science has shown that the microbes can combine some of the metals with other elements creating a nontoxic gas that will volatize away. The EPA is doing its job and the heavy metals in the sewage systems are being cleaned up so well that a lot of the *vivo* can be used *as is* without restrictions. Because of restrictions limiting the amount of heavy metals that industry can put into sewage systems, the resulting sludge is much cleaner and safer than it was only a few years ago. Sludge is, however, full of nutrient minerals. As a result, you need to test the soil to make sure you do not overload it with minerals.

The most sensible way to handle sludge is to compost it with the mountains of brush, yard waste, pallets, paper and other organic carbon materials that are filling up the scarce landfills. The microbes, nitrogen and other nutrients and moisture in *vivo* are the missing ingredients, the perfect match, to make the finest compost in the world out of huge amount of trash. The composting action would guarantee the *vivo* compost to be free of dangerous pathogens. Any heavy metals the *vivo* could contain would be vastly diluted and some would be turned into a harmless gas and released into the air. Tests have shown composted *vivo* to actually be lower in heavy metals than some commercial fertilizers, even some considered organic. In areas where a lot of *vivo* is produced but carbon materials to compost with it are scarce, it still needs to be used. It is too valuable to be wasted. It can be applied directly to the land, but more care and testing will have to be done than when it is composted.

COMPOST TEAS

Compost solubles, leachates or tea are all terms describing the best part of the compost. Don't let them go to waste. We purposely do static piles pushed up ten to twelve feet high so the piles can soak up our average rainfall without any leaching out the bottom that could then wash away. In 1987, we got almost double our annual rain. In one 24-hour period alone we got ten inches, and the tea started running out the bottom of our piles. I wasn't able to capture and bottle it, so I trenched it toward a pecan grove nearby.

The years 1988 and 1989 were very dry. We were eight and ten inches below the annual rainfall in my area. The farmers around us were making poor hay crops, if they made any at all. The Johnsongrass grew up head tall both years in the area I drained the leachates to. I kept mowing it off and it kept growing right back. I could have made three good hay crops each year from that spot.

To this day, eight years later, that spot is still as rich as it was in 1988. The grass is still growing much thicker, greener and healthier than any in the surrounding area. The pecan trees in that spot are also doing better. The trees look better than other trees on the place, the leaves are bigger and darker green and trees themselves are bigger than the other trees.

All organic materials have to be disassembled, broken down and digested by microbes before they become food for plants. The solubles the water leaches out of well-made compost are the dissolved minerals, microbe exudates, dead microbes, live microbes, hormones and many unknown ingredients that not only feed the plants but can actually help in controlling diseases and insects when sprayed on the plants.

Compost tea can be used to water the roots or used as a foliar feed by spraying the leaves. Use a strong tea when applying to the soil. Use it weak, about the color of iced tea, when spraying on the leaves. It is always best to spray in the cool of the morning. On vegetables and other fast-growing plants you can apply to foliage and/or soil once a week. For slow-growing houseplants, you can apply the same way, but use only once a month.

Using Compost

Back home on the farm when I was a kid, and now on my own farm, we just spread the manure and other waste on the land in the fall. We put it on the stubble after the crops were out and immediately worked it in shallow with a disk harrow. Up until that time we kept it in piles shaped to shed rain and keep the nutrients from being leached away by water or air. If that material had seeds or diseases we didn't want to transfer to the fields, we would let the pile soak up some rain or wet it if the season was dry and let it compost a while. We didn't have a means of turning the piles other than by hand, which was too much work, so we just added some clean material on top for insulation so the inside could all heat up and compost.

Pathogens that attack plants and animals can't compete with the composting microbes, and even if the pile doesn't get real hot the bad pathogens are destroyed along with the unwanted seeds. From experience I have learned the soil benefits greatly if the composting action is completed in the top few inches of the soil. That is where Nature does it; however, if raw or unfinished compost is applied heavily, the decomposing microbes can interfere with growing crops. You will need to wait until the decomposers have done their work, which may be one to twelve weeks depending on volume, particle size, carbon-nitrogen ratio and the richness of the soil on which it is applied.

AN UPHILL BATTLE

Nature is crying for help. Compost could be her rescue. Except for a few, our land grant universities have mostly ignored her. I gave a presentation to a dairy group on the value and long-term benefits of spreading manure on agricultural soils. The speaker who followed me was an agriculture Ph.D. His first words from the podium were, "Gentlemen, we have to face it. If you have to haul manure across the road or more than a mile or two, it isn't worth the effort. It only has twenty pounds of nitrogen per ton."

On another occasion a wealthy man attended a presentation I gave and ordered a 60 cubic yard load of compost. Before we had a chance to deliver, he called and canceled. He said his county ag agent was having a fit. The ag agent told him compost would bring in diseases, insects and all kinds of pests. He also said the nitrates would keep the trees green too long in the fall and then they would freeze. These two college-educated gentlemen should have studied more in Nature instead of in the classroom. They would have gotten a better education.

One of my employees, an ex-pro ball player, has three children who also excel in sports. He approached their school and suggested they spread compost on their ball fields. Not only would they save water and fertilizer but the turf would be thicker and softer which could also help prevent injuries. He was rejected with, "Oh no, our students would get disease and infections from compost." I fail to see their logic, especially since they apply all types of toxic pesticides and chemicals to the turf for those kids to play in. These are not isolated incidences. We have experienced this ignorance many times and so have other composters and organic growers.

We have since spent a few thousand dollars with a well-respected microbiologist on testing. He found no disease-causing organisms. To some this research still wasn't convincing. There seems to be a mindset that anything dead or of animal residue is awful and should be disposed of at a dump that is not near their backyard. The research also discovered that 27% of the isolates were insect pathogens, and another 18% of the isolates were important in the bioremediation of environmental pollutants. Compost tea is now being used to help control the imported fire ant and is also being used as a fungicide.

Bioremediation is nothing more than selective composting. If given enough time the microbes in a well-constructed compost pile can disassemble any toxin man has put together. Compost should be used on athletic fields and on any lawn where children play, especially if toxic pesticides have been used there in the past. Compost will help clean up the damage that has been done through the use of toxic chemicals. Our kids are in much more danger from them than they are from good, clean soil.

Because the testing proved there were no harmful pathogens in the compost, we have finally seen it used on two football fields. The results are so good that other athletic directors are requesting compost for their playing fields.

We have since ended up with a bonus in our sales pitch. The teams that play on the two football fields we composted both won the state championships of 1995 class 5A.

DEMONSTRATING COMPOST

Some people have to be shown. Our county agricultural extension service hired a new, young agent fresh out of college. He and I soon became good friends. For years I tried to get the agent to use some of my compost. He wouldn't buy any and he wouldn't let me give him some to try. His answer was always, "Beck, compost is a good mulch — I believe in mulches but compost is too low in nutrients, you still have to use fertilizers."

I waited and waited for an opportunity to get the agent to give compost a test. Finally I found a way to trick him into trying it. The competitor making compost at the feedlot was discussing his poor sales with me one day and asked how we could boost sales. At first I didn't want to tell a competitor how to sell, then a thought struck me. The new county agent needs to know about our compost. I told the competitor to take some of his compost to the agent's house and tell him I sent him.

When he arrived at the agent's house and announced that Beck had sent him, the agent with mixed emotions said, "That damn Beck! All right, dump it right there on the lawn and I'll haul it out to the garden."

A few weeks later the agent called and said, "Beck come over here. I want to show you something." When I got there I immediately saw why he called. There was a thick, dark green spot in his lawn that made the rest of the yard look bad, and even the neighbors' lawns look poor. The agent came out of the house and said, "That spot bogs my lawn mower down, and when I am late in watering, the rest of the lawn wilts. The

128   *The Secret Life of Compost*

taller green spot doesn't wilt, and it seems like it should wilt first. I can find it by walking across it in the dark it is so thick." Then he said, "Beck, if you can duplicate that you won't have enough compost to sell."

I called my competitor and told him we got the new agent's attention and he was going to allow us to do a test on his lawn under his supervision. We each took a yard of compost and spread it a half-inch thick and watered it in. We did this in a location where everything such as shade, slope and water would be the same, and we kept a control area between the two composted spots.

This test just happened to be in the fall of the year. The two composted spots came out beautiful and green while the control spot and the rest of the lawn went dormant. That was in 1983 when a long, severe freeze hit at Christmas time. The agent called me and predicted the two green composted spots would be killed because they were actively growing while the rest of the lawn was dormant. But come spring, the two composted spots came out first and with no freeze damage while the rest of the lawn had damage.

Needless to say, my compost sales did go up a bunch. A few months later, the agent called me again and said, "Beck, be there, I am bringing you an article to read." It was a story in a turf journal about a researcher using compost on a lawn in the fall. He applied the same thickness, watered it in just like we did and got the same results. Since then there has been a tremendous amount of research done with compost, all getting excellent results in growth, disease suppression and insect resistance. The lawns always withstood weather stresses better and required less, and in some cases much less, irrigation.

To illustrate the water savings I want to tell of a friend who put *vivo* compost on his lawn. While he was out spreading the compost his neighbor looked over and asked, "Jim what are you spreading?" Jim replied, "Dillo Dirt." The neighbor asked, "What is Dillo Dirt?" Jim replied, "Austin sludge." With that, the neighbor got a frown on his face and said, "I don't think I approve of that."

Time went by; the hot dry summer months came. The neighbor's lawn, which had topsoil and chemicals applied to it in the spring, looked awful, while Jim's lawn looked great. Jim couldn't wait to brag to the neighbor. Finally he caught the neighbor outside. "My lawn looks much better than yours," he said. The neighbor replied, "It sure does, and my water bill is killing me. It has been in excess of $200 the past two months." Jim was ashamed to tell him that his own water bill was $38 and $42 those two months. The neighbor said he had to water every day to try and keep his lawn from wilting; Jim only watered once a week. The two yards were the same size. The neighbor and his wife lived in their house, whereas Jim had a wife and two young daughters living in their house. The excessive water bill had to be a result of watering the lawn.

COMPOST & WATER CONSERVATION

Cool, clear water, you don't miss it until the well goes dry. No life can exist without it. Man must have it in a pure and fresh condition.

A rich composted soil covered with alive and/or decaying plant matter is Nature's water filter and regulator, and it also determines the quantity and quality of the water in our wells.

An organic mulch cover holds heavy rains in place, giving it time to soak in. Later, when the hot, dry seasons come it keeps water from evaporating back to the atmosphere.

Sticky substances are exuded by the microbes as they break down the organic materials on and in the soil. This sticky substance glues the fine, powdery soil particles together to form a fine crumb structure. This crumb structure allows carbon dioxide and oxygen exchange necessary for healthy root growth and the proliferation of the beneficial soil life that controls the pathogens in the soil.

The crumb structure also allows better water insoak from rain, especially heavy rains. Research has shown that a soil with a 4 to 5% organic matter can soak up a 6 inch rain where and when it falls.

Most of our soils can now only soak up about one half of what they should. Water that soaks into the soil is held in the humus and clay of the soil for future plant use. Any amount of insoak water the soil can't hold is filtered by the organic matter of the soil as it continues on down to feed the aquifers that supply drinking water and keep the springs flowing at a constant rate instead of periodically going dry. Heavy rain on soils lacking in organic matter with no crumb structure can't accept the water. It then runs off carrying along soil and increasing the volume of flood water which rushes to the streams, then the rivers, causing damaging floods.

Instead of studying nature and taking a close look for the cause of floods, human, not-too-brilliant reasoning sees only rain as the problem. The true cause of bad flooding is ignored and large dams are built to collect the flood water in lakes. Now more energy is being waisted to pump the water back to the farm land where it should have remained.

While the soil carried by the flooding waters collects at the bottom of the lakes, each new flood gradually fills the lakes with more soil until, eventually, they become big mud holes.

MORE SECRETS OF COMPOST

Compost is nature's finest soil conditioner. Compost is also her finest fertilizer, although not recognized as such by the fertilizer industry because the N, P and K doesn't add up to a total of at least 21. Compost is the decomposing remains of many once-live entities. Through the decay processes of composting the life forces and necessary elements can be passed from one generation of life to the next. Little, if any extra plant foods need to be added to the soil.

When N, P, K and other minerals are added to the soil the microbes must work on and release them in correct conditions for healthy plant growth. To do this the microbes must have an energy source. Decaying organic matter furnishes the energy and nutrients for microbes to balance out the plant foods in the soil.

The roots take in the nutrients and transport them throughout the plant in solutions through the vascular system. In order for the solutions to move upward the leaves transpire, or lose, moisture out of the pores called stomata.

If the solutions are lacking and not balanced with nutrients the plants must continue to lose moisture out of the leaves until enough nutrients are carried up. If the solutions are loaded with a balance of nutrients less moisture is needed for transportation resulting in less moisture lost. In rich organic soils the plant will actually require less water to grow even though rich organic soils can hold more moisture than poor soils. Adding chemical salt fertilizers to soils that are low in organic matter causes plants to require more water while growing.

Compost is the material that performs all of these miracles. Compost is the champion of water conservation. If the composting process is on and/or in the soil under a plant canopy it does still more.

Carbon is an essential part of all life. It is the basic building block for all plant life. Carbon is the most abundant element in the compost pile. The decay organisms combine the carbon in compost with oxygen from the air to make carbon dioxide (CO_2) gas.

Plants must have CO_2 for photosynthesis to make carbohydrates. It has been calculated that a one acre field of grain or an acre grove of orange trees uses over 6 tons of carbon dioxide annually. The air only contains 0.03% carbon dioxide.

Still, a bag of modern chemical fertilizer labeled "complete" will not list carbon. Of the ingredients listed, nitrogen will be first. And it is usually the highest number. The same air that has only .03% carbon dioxide will contain 78% nitrogen. Plants also use nitrogen from the air. Bacteria are the agents by which 90% of needed nitrogen of the air is converted to useful compounds for plants. To do that work the bacteria use the energy that is stored in the carbon rich materials of compost.

Are we putting the wrong stuff in bags and feeding the wrong thing to the soil for the plants to use?

Science has known for some time that with an abundance or ample carbon dioxide in the air plants utilized water more efficiently. Plants breath through the stomata (tiny pores) on the leaf surface. They breathe in carbon dioxide, take out the carbon and release the oxygen. Plants also transpire water through the stomata. In hot, dry weather conditions the plant wants to cut down on water loss so the stomata closes as soon as the leaf has absorbed enough carbon dioxide. If carbon dioxide concentrations are low, the stomata must stay open long periods and the plant loses excess water. If there are higher concentrations of CO_2, the stomata quickly absorb enough carbon dioxide for photosynthesis, allowing them to stay closed for longer periods.

A soil covered with decaying mulch, compost or containing an abundance of decaying organic matter will be giving off a lot of CO_2 from the microbe decaying activity. Carbon dioxide is slightly heavier than air, so it hovers near the soil before it diffuses into the atmosphere. All plants, especially lawn grasses, row crops and small plants next to the soil surface can make efficient use of the extra CO_2, resulting in better growth.

With energy and nutrients from compost the microbes can quickly furnish plants with all minerals, including carbon, with much less water being pulled from the soil lessening the need for rain or irrigation.

At the same time the microbes will be converting the nitrogen from the air to a form the plants can use.

There are many reasons contributing to the benefits of spreading compost on lawns, flower beds, farms and orchards or wherever plants grow — soil conditioning, aerating, water insoak, water retention and conservation, higher nutrition, soil life stimulation, beneficial microbes that attack insects and diseases, ion exchange, air nitrogen conversion, release of CO_2 in the correct location, air purifying, and many more not yet discovered benefits. The main reason compost works so well is it is Nature's way. She designed decay and has been composting since her beginning.

The Judge

A Master Designer created Mother Nature and authored the Natural Laws. We had no part in making, designing or enacting a single rule. We are only part of Nature. We cannot change, alter or break any of the laws without causing harm to ourselves.

Everything in Nature (even what we call waste) is designed to be perfect and has a purpose. We are the highest beings on earth, so everything on earth was designed to be of service and aid to us. If we studied from this approach we would learn things, make discoveries, and see things otherwise blocked from view.

The future of a livable existence on earth hinges on our knowing and obeying the natural laws. If we allow the environment to rule and Mother Nature to judge, our existence on earth could only improve.

We too were designed to be perfect . . . except the Master Designer gave us free will.

Greed, envy and jealousy — all traits of human free will — seem to influence public policy, sway bureaucracy and taint our written laws. They even decide where to place sewer plants, landfills, and the compost operations demanded by Nature to recycle the huge amounts of waste we create. Placing these entities could be the easiest decision to make if geology and environment were studied and Nature was given first consideration and allowed to rule.

True, no one wants these sites in their backyards, but we all create waste and it has to go someplace. Moving these sites too far creates pollution from vehicle wear and exhaust. Noise, dust, traffic and strong odors are also created in proportion to distance material has to be transported.

Those who live near naturally selected sites should somehow be compensated. I think cutting property taxes or utilities to the degree of nuisances being tolerated would be fair compensation. All other citizens (who also create waste) but who do not have the nuisance should pick up the difference.

When Nature points to the location to place these entities, politics should not be able to overrule.

SEVEN LAWS OF SUCCESS

Whether you are composting for your own garden or on a commercial scale, whether you are a serious farmer or a weekend gardener, you will find that working with Nature has many rewards. I have found in my experience that following these seven laws in every area of life helps me live more fully and more contentedly. They have grown from my experience with life and Nature. I share them with you in the hope that they will bring you the satisfaction they have brought me.

1. DO NOT ABUSE YOUR BODY.

Keep your body and mind in the best of health. A stressed body cannot be fully productive or nourish a creative and sound mind. Hate and negative thoughts of any degree destroy the mind and the body.

2. USE YOUR TALENTS.

Pursue an occupation that you enjoy, regardless of what it is, as long as it is good. Every person on earth has a God-given talent to do something beneficial that he or she can enjoy and prosper from. The only difference between work and play is the degree of enjoyment you have while doing it. It is easy to have fun and a good attitude doing a job that you like. Don't let pay scale drive you into an occupation you will not be happy in. All successful and prosperous people are doing work they love.

3. STUDY, STUDY, STUDY.

If you want to accomplish something, you must look at the problem or question from every angle and point of view. Read books, go to school. Discuss your ideas with other people. Even if you think the person you are talking with knows nothing about the subject, talk about it anyway. The other person may spark a thought that leads to success.

4. ASK GOD FOR HELP.

And most importantly, have faith that you will receive the help you need. The help may not come in the way you wish, but you will receive what is best. From my earliest childhood I had dreams of the many things I wanted to do and to have, and I put these dreams into my subconscious without the slightest doubt that they would come to me. At the right time, they all materialized — the jobs, the wife, the children, the business, the knowledge, the accomplishments, the awards, the acquaintances, the house, the farm, the big trees, the big trucks and tractors, and even patents. I cannot think of a single dream I didn't get by following these seven positive laws.

5. THINK FOR YOURSELF.

Accept the word of others as neither true nor false. Listen and store what others think and see if or how it fits and is proven by your own ideas and experience.

6. DON'T GIVE UP.

See the big picture; consider setbacks and hardships as necessary learning experiences. Always think positively, and never, never think negatively. There is some good in every person and something to be learned from every event. The good only needs searching for.

7. THANK GOD.

If what you wish for is good and you have faith, it will come. And when you share your beneficial knowledge and discoveries, you will prosper much greater than if you selfishly kept them hidden. Knowledge and discoveries don't belong to any one person; they are eternal. They are written for all by the Master Designer. Just feel honored to be a chosen messenger. And if you wish for future requests to be granted, you must not forget the last law of success — and that is to tell God thanks!

Afterword

On one occasion during Socrates-like sessions with the late William A. Albrecht, the great professor handed off an insight I remember to this day. I had asked him, "Is there such a thing as a sure-fire fertilizer?" His answer came back, not like a rifle shot, but more like a word from a patient teacher to a less-than-brilliant pupil.

"You turn in a crop similar to the one you want to grow. If you want to grow a cereal crop, then turn in rye. The cell structure of the fertilizer crop has more intelligence about plant nutrition than all the Ph.D.'s in North America."

The term *intelligence* was used by Albrecht quite deliberately. He was not confusing intelligence with intellect. For the expression of intelligence can take place at the cellular, sub-cellular or tissue level, or — as in human beings — at the level of the central nervous system. In fact, it can be noted that intelligence is universal in character. The Creator has decreed that intelligence does not operate from the brain alone, or even chiefly. Even the so-called dead stone in a field has its ordered intelligence, bestowed in its atomic arrangement and molecular design. The orbit of its electrons and the construction of its molecules give us an observed density, color and texture — not to dwell on its nutrient makeup. These are a gift of the intelligence that towers over all from the lightest element to the far out galaxies. From this point of view, the compost pile no doubt contains more innate intelligence than the entire work force at USDA. The beautiful planet on which we live is but a small speck hung in its proper place among the planets and the stars of the universe.

The Indian physician and philosopher, Depack Chopra, points with great clarity to the observation that everything we comprehend through our senses is an expression of the organizing power of knowledge. We must be humbled, indeed, when we realize that the grand miscellany of Nature is a complex of universal thought from which we can extract a few fragments of knowledge.

The intelligence Albrecht spoke of operates in every cell of the body, human or animal. It operates in the blade of grass or the soaring branches of a California redwood — everywhere.

Synthesis in the laboratory, therefore, has to appear to Nature as an attempt to imitate Nature, an effort about as clumsy as a dinosaur attempting to build a pocket watch.

A created intelligence pervades the finite world in which we live, and the human mind is also an expression of this intelligence. The thirst for an understanding of God is as much a part of our DNA blueprint as the groping for what we call scientific truth.

How elusive and blundersome — if we can excuse that term — some parts of scientific progress can get is illustrated, I hope, in the short scenario that follows.

On another occasion, I was visiting with the late Ted Whitmer of Glendive, Montana. Ted grew up on the family farm, his earliest recollection being that of a less-than-teenage cowboy. Through the years he made himself one of the best educated men I have ever met. A world that sees dilution as a solution cannot live at the level of its great men, Ted Whitmer being one of them.

Ted helped me make the human disease-soil connection, and it ties back to our failing to recycle, compost and preserve the fertility of the soil — all in homage to the god called science.

The recorded beginning for the contamination model now being used by most farmers harks back to the day and hour phosphate fertilizers — bagged and dutifully labeled according to Fertilizer Institute and state law standards — became state-of-the-art fare for the production of basic storable commodities. It was known, of course, that hardly 9-12% of these phosphates were taken up by crops. Nevertheless, liberal applications spawned a fantastic sales ticket, distributed the fluoride by-product, and ultimately underwrote the contamination of the water supply in the name of dental care. Not clearly understood by most farmers outside of eco-agriculture circles is the fact that only a small measure of the fertilizer fluoride in parent materials is removed by the firing process. Inserted into the soil with each bag of acid-treated phosphate fertilizer is enough fluoride to bowl over a herd of cattle.

As with many other contamination problems, dilution is perceived to be the solution. So fluoride rides along as an inert component of the fertilizer sack, leaving nature to deal with the problem once the disk and drill have passed over the field.

The above having been said, we now have to add that the phosphate-fluoride connection follows the food chain. Just about everyone will admit that phosphate as taken from the rock contains 1.5-3% fluoride in the parent material. World phosphate deposits in fact, run from 1.5-9% fluoride. These deposits are hardly processed. They are put through the kiln to drive off enough fluorine so the product can be used to replace bone meal in cow, dog and chicken feed, etc. The high level of fluoride in the rock enters the food chain via the grain. A hand-held calculator can figure the amount of fluoride gifted to the crop each time forty pounds of phosphate fertilizers are added to an acre. Fluoride ends up in the bran. It is reasonable to figure several pounds of fluoride are in thirty bushels of wheat.

Withal, the food and water supply now runs from 8 to 50 and 80 ppm fluoride. We can extend this inventory of information into the nation's health profile.

Fluoride displaces iodine because it is a halogen. Iodine resides in the thyroid gland, and in its absence the thyroid gland does not manufacture thyroxin. In the absence of thyroxin, there is no oxidation of sugar in the cells. With sugars unoxidized, fermentation becomes automatic. Lactic acids are formed. Lactic acid, of course, is abundant in all malignant tissues. When fermentation is not the end product, fat is.

This inventory of information should have public health officials asking, "Why in the devil are we adding fluoride to the water?" This while authorities argue about adding fluoride to the water at 1 to 1.5 ppm.

We can suggest a compost connection here because there are enough phosphates in most soils to last until the next ice age. This nutrient and others cannot be mobilized, however, when the soil system is allowed to fall into disrepair.

A fair measure of that repair always depends on compost, whether delivered as green manure, decayed stover, with suitable air and water management, or as recycled carbonaceous materials generated by the environment and the civilization in which we live. This also explains why some farmers experience drought while at the same time neighbors across the country road have ample water for their crops.

Mankind's attempts to synthesize nature via fertility manufacture, rescue chemistry, all while wastes accumulate and men decay, seems to author degenerative metabolic disease and destruction of that thin layer of topsoil that nurtures us all.

We know, even though we cannot comprehend, that a single sperm cell united with an ovum can produce the complex mechanism called the human body, each blueprint direction and thought pattern programmed in a multi-minuscule DNA filled with trillions of commands and billions of options. To think that everything is "alive" with an equally awesome manual for operation is a wonderment we can understand best by obeying.

The secret life of the compost pile and the farmer's use thereof is a fulfillment, as is always the case with a great work of art.

— *Charles Walters*

Index

fly parasites, commercially available, 109
foliar feeding, with compost tea, 123
food chain, 13, 18, 21, 118, 142
food-processing plants, 92
food supply, 142
football fields, use of compost on, 127-128
forced-air windrows, 99
forest floor, as example of compost, 59, 92, 116
fossil fuel, 5-6
four-way soil mix, selling, 114
freeze damage, prevention of, 128
fruit, 25, 65
fungal attack, 7
fungi, 22-23
fungicide, compost tea as, 127

gambling, 34
Garcia, Eddy, 114-115
garden bed, 87
garden soil, selling, 114
gasoline, 43, 76
gated charge hopper, 82
gene pool, 7
gin waste, 60
global warming, 41
God, 14, 32, 135-136, 138-140
grain, 55, 133, 142
grass, 48; clippings, 115-116; dry, 48
green materials, 48
grinder, 69, 101-102; slow-speed, 72; small, 102; tub, 68-70
grinding drum, 73
ground water, 60
guar seed, 48
gum wood, 68
gypsum board, 69

halogen, 142
hammers, in grinders, 69, 73, 102
hauling, 86
hay, 51, 60, 101, 122; cane, 59; grass, 48; legume, 48
health, human, 65, 136, 142; public, 142; soil, plant and animal, 20; soil, plant and animal, 21
health department, 93
heavy metals, amount in vivo, 122; dilution of, 119; problems with, 118; removal of, 121
herbicides, 8, 26, 41
highway engineers, 97
home gardening, 47, 87, 89, 106, 112,118, 136
hoof and horn meal, 48
hormones, in compost tea, 123
houseplants, and compost tea application, 123
Howard, Sir Albert, 20-21
hulls, 60

human health, 7
human body, 118
human disease-soil connection, 141
humus, 14, 17, 19, 25, 41, 56, 60, 131
hunting hounds, 49
hydrogen, 5, 8
hydrophobic material, 101

in-vessel composting method, 98
industry, 55
infections, risk to humans from compost, 127
inoculant, for compost, 119
insect pathogens, found in compost, 127
insect resistance, increased by compost, 129
insects, control of, 35, 70, 123, 134; pests, 7, 25, 126
institutions, research, 106
iodine, displaced by fluoride, 142
ion exchange, 134
iron ore, 34
irrigation, 22, 58, 64, 91, 129, 134

Johnsongrass, 61, 122

kitchen scraps, 48, 51, 53
knives, in grinders, 69, 73, 102
Kowalski, Bill, 23

lab tests, 106
lactic acids, 142
land grant universities, 126
landfill, 15, 18, 27, 34, 55, 93, 96, 112, 121, 136
landscape soil, selling, 114
landscapers, 73, 91-92, 114
Latin America, 7
lawn care, 106-107, 127-128, 134
lawn grasses, 134
lawn mower, 50, 128
leachates, 50
leaching, 98, 122
lead paint, 69
leather meal, 48
leaves, 48; dried, 48; shredding, 116
legumes, 56, 62-63
lime, 68, 97
limestone, for compost pad, 96-97
Limits of Growth, The, 35
liquid waste, 76
liquid brewery waste, 77
loader, 75, 96, 101, 104; all-wheel drive, 103; used for turning, 104
loading, 80-82, 85
Lowdermilk, Walter, 35

machete, 50

pine bark, as mulch, 117-118
pine wood, as truck bed liner, 79
plastic bags, problems with in composting materials, 116
plastics, 33, 68
plow, 52
plowing, 91
Poirot, Gene, 32
pollution, 5, 47, 65; automobile, 42, 136; bioremediation of through compost use, 127; from trucking, 118; of ground water, 60; noise, 42; of surface water, 60
potassium, 8, 52, 60
potting mixes, 107
potting soil, developing, 115; selling, 114
power plant, by-products of, 97
price-setting, 113
private enterprise, 113
protein, 7, 41, 44, 60, 107, 118
public health, 142
pump, retention pond, 76
pumping, in irrigation, 131

racetrack stable bedding, 71
railroad, 91
rain, 17, 22, 42, 52, 61-62, 64, 96, 98-100, 117, 122, 125, 130, 134
raw compost, 126
redwood trees, 140
reincarnation, 4
reproduction, animal, 19
research grants, 107
retention pond, 68, 76, 109
retirement homes, marketing to, 112
rhizosphere, 24
rice, 7; brown, whole grain, 19-20; polished, white 19-20
robber flies, for fly control, 109
rock, 17; fluoride in, 142; mineral, 17
rock powders, 64
rocks, problems with in composting materials, 105
Rodale, J.I., v
Rodale, Robert, 61
rodents, 51
roller, sheepfoot, 68
roots, 21-24, 26, 40, 42, 50, 63-64, 123; and nutrient transport, 132; and temperature sensitivity, 117; healthy growth of, 131; problems with in composted material, 105
root rot, 23-24; cotton, 63
roses, growing, 114; tea, 115
row crops, 134
runoff, 68
rust, problems with, 105
rye, 63, 139; elbon, 63

salts, 42; in soil, 60
salt water, removing odor with, 107
San Antonio, x, 43, 113, 115, 118
sand, 92; selling, 114
sawdust, 48, 74- 75, 96, 108, 119
scientists, 31
scrap iron, 34
screen, 68, 70, 72, 81, 104; small, 102; home-made, 80, 84; portable, 80-81; stainless steel, 82, 84, 105; stationary, 80; trammel, 82; vibrating, 80
screening compost, 100, 106
screens, size and variety of, 105
Seattle, Chief, 9
sedimentation, 6
seed hulls, 48
seed meal, 48
seeds, 125; problems with in composted material, 105
Seven Laws for Success, 112, 136-138
sewage sludge, 86
sewage treatment plant, 95, 118, 121, 136
sewer plants, 27
sewer systems, 53
sheepfoot roller, 68
shingles, asphalt, 69
shipping, 100
shrubs, 92, 106
Sierra Blanca experiment, 120
sludge, sewage, 53, 55, 86, 95, 118-120; as inoculant, 119
soil aeration, 134
soil, alkaline, 62
Soil and Soil Science, 57
soil blends, special, 113
soil compaction, 60
soil conditioners, 118, 134
soil formation, 14, 17
soil mixes, 114
soil nutrition, 134
soil testing, 60, 63, 88, 121
soybean seed, 48
spores, 22
spraying, 26
sprinkler, 76, 117
sprouting seeds, 107
stable bedding, 74, 101
stables, horse, 92
stainless steel, used in screen building, 82, 84, 105
static-pile composting method, 67, 71, 75, 86, 98-99, 102, 116, 119, 122
steel truck bed, problems with, 79
stockyards, 59
stomata, 132-134
stover, 143
straw, 48

stumps, 69, 73, 102
styrofoam cups, problems with in composting material, 104
Sudangrass, 62
sugar, oxidation of, 142
sun, 23, 34
sunlight, 8, 22, 32
surface water, 60
swallows, for fly control, 109
symbiosis, 22

tanker truck, 76-77
taxes, 113; property, 97, 136
teflon, as liner for trailer, 80
temperature, 44, 117; effected by application of sludge, 120; in compost, 98, 119, 125; lower under mulch, 117
termites, 70
testing compost, 106
Texas, 4, 48, 86; east, 99; high plains of, 21; hill country of, 23; west, 95, 120; west, as sight of vivo-spreading operation, 87
Texas A&M University, 25
The Soil and Health, 20
Thompson, Louis M., 57
thyroid gland, 142
thyroxin, 142
tomato cage, 89
tomato juice, removing odor with, 107
topsoil, 17, 18, 92, 96; application of, 130; destruction of, 143; erosion of, 19; weed-fee mixes, 114
toxic rescue chemistry, 7, 27, 56, 143
trace elements, 52
trace minerals, 33
track hoe, 69
tractor, crawler, 60; used to turn compost, 72; used to change screen drums, 83; with enlarged bucket, 77; with homemade boom, 83
tractors, compaction caused by, 104; engines of, 103; size of, 103
tractor tires, used as planters, 88
trade, 34
traffic, problems with, 136; truck and tractor, 96
trailer, 81; aluminum, 80
trammel screen, 82, 105
trammels, 80
transpiration, 132
tree trimmings, 70, 86, 95, 101
trees, 106; cedar, 70; evergreen, 97; hackberry, 39; orange, 133; pecan, 25, 122; redwood, 4, 140; risk of freezing, 126
truck beds, best kind of, 79; problems with, 78-79; wood-lined, pine, 79
trucking, 92, 100, 118; expense of, 96

trucks, 82; loading of, 104; tanker, 76-77; with gate and chain for spreading, 85
tub grinders, 68-70
turning compost, 72, 99, 102, 104, 108, 116

USDA, 6-7, 35, 140
university research, 107
urine, 71, 101

vascular system, 132
vegetable waste, 74, 108
vegetables, 55, 64-65, 74, 91, 106, 123; composting, 108
vermicomposting, 52
vermiculite, selling, 114
vetch, Lana, 63
vineyards, 59, 118
vesicles, 22
vivo, 86-87, 122, 130; definition of, 121
Voisin, Andre, 33

walking floor van, 71
Walters, Charles, *v*, 120
waste candy, 73
water, added to compost piles, 98; drinking, 131
water commission, 93
water conservation, 113, 126, 128-130, 132-134
water insoak, 131, 134
water retention, 134
water supply, 141-142
watergun, 76
weeds, 7, 48, 62; control of, 35, 65, 92
weed seeds, 59
Weniger, Del, *v*, *x*
wheat, 142
Whitmer, Ted, 141
wind, 17; direction of, 108; problems with, 97
windrow turners, 98-101, 104
windrows, 71, 75, 99; forced-air, 99; size of, 101
wire, for screens, 105
wire cages, 51
wood, gum, 68; oak, 68
wood chips, 48, 116
wood-lined truck bed, pine, 79
wood shavings, 101
word-of-mouth marketing, 111
yard trimmings, 95, 99, 118-119
yard waste, 121

zoning, 96